ALSO BY NIGEL CALDER

Technopolis
The Violent Universe
The Mind of Man
The Restless Earth
The Life Game
The Weather Machine
The Human Conspiracy
The Key to the Universe
Spaceships of the Mind
Einstein's Universe
Nuclear Nightmares
The Comet Is Coming!
Timescale
1984 and Beyond
The English Channel

EDITOR

Unless Peace Comes
Nature in the Round

THE GREEN MACHINES

Nigel Calder

G. P. PUTNAM'S SONS / New York

G. P. Putnam's Sons
Publishers Since 1838
200 Madison Avenue
New York, NY 10016

Library of Congress Cataloging-in-Publication Data

Calder, Nigel.
  The green machines.

  Bibliography: p.
  1. Biotechnology. 2. Agricultural biotechnology.
I. Title.
TP248.2.C35 1986   303.4'9   86–12188
ISBN 0–399–13176–0

Printed in the United States of America
1 2 3 4 5 6 7 8 9 10

CONTENTS

1 BEFORE THE REVOLUTION

HOPE tiptoed back into the world, armed with sachets of benign bacteria. Late in the twentieth century the threat of nuclear war, sustained by self-appointed masters of the planet, darkened everyone's future, and the computer models of nuclear winter spread soot and despair all around the Earth. Biological science then put the remedy into the hands of ordinary people.

It was hope of a cynical kind, but all the stronger for that. The new biotechnology, orchestrated in green machines, introduced novel means of producing more abundant food, energy, and raw materials, from sunlight and living resources available anywhere. More by accident than design, they also offered a way of surviving a nuclear war. Communities with green machines would be able to scorn the generals and politicians, and treat the man-made risk of nuclear war as if it were a nasty but survivable natural hazard, akin to an earthquake or an epidemic. People Power, expressing itself in practical self-protection, would topple the world's governments and replace the nation-states by a network of self-reliant villages.

The human species was sleepwalking toward the revolution. That is why this book is written in the past tense, even though it concerns an imminent future. Historical facts and extant speculations from scientists and social reformers furnish most of what needs to be said. The past tense avoids the quarrels between "will," "may," and "should" that bedevil writings about the future, and helps to divorce the analysis from current pontifications of Left, Right and even Green politicians. Transformation for survival will be strong in practical politics and weak in theory—more like the American Revolution than the Russian. Its best slogan may be, "No speeches!"

The somnambulists of the 1980s were led by those who were applying rudimentary biotechnology in rural areas, and the state of play in various regions of the world is the subject of Part 1. In Part 2, researchers in industrial and academic labs are observed hard at work, developing more powerful forms of green machinery with the help of genetic engineering and other novelties. These make the old utopian dream of self-reliant communities realistic at last, and in Part 3 decentralization appears as the escape from the death trap of a world of nation-states made far too powerful by perverted science. But dreamers, on waking up, have to reassess their opportunity hardheadedly, judging it against modern perceptions of human nature and the realities of military power.

A Postscript embodies, in fictional form, the author's answer to the question: "How do we get from here to there?" It tells the story of the Winter Farms in a post-revolutionary perspective. Indeed the book as a whole distances itself from contemporary events. It looks back on the present as if from the standpoint of our successors, who will gasp with pity at the bizarre existence of people who paid taxes to distant leaders and granted them powers of life and death.

The Village in the Computer

When the East India Company set up a trading post at Madras in the sixteenth century, to buy prized chintzes from Indian craftsmen, it began the intrusion that led to the British usurping the Indians' weaving industry. Three and a half centuries later a computer in Scotland was making some amends. The Energy Studies Unit of the University of Strathclyde in Glasgow used computer models to figure out biotechnological policies for villages of the Coromandel Coast south of Madras, in the hope that economic advancement in rural India might pick up from where deliberate deindustrialization had left it. It made one small village famous worldwide, among people looking for better roads to rural development in the poorest countries.

Injambakkam was the name of the village, but there were two versions. In one, beside the blue Bay of Bengal, Indians harvested their rice and grieved for infants who had not lived to eat it. The other Injambakkam, on the banks of the gray river Clyde, was populated by electronic impulses immune to human sentiment and squabbles, and its harvest was computer printout. Each village was a pale shadow of the other. The one on the Coromandel Coast had the sunshine, garlands, and kingfishers, but its inhabitants were poorer and did not eat half as well as their counterparts in the computer.

Chris Lewis, the microbiologist who was chief elder of the electronic Injambakkam in Scotland, liked to quote Mao Tse-tung's dictum: "Industry must develop with agriculture." For the two million more or less impoverished villages of the Third World the key to economic development, in Lewis's view, would be a matching of biotechnology to the local ecosystem of each village in such a way as to make it self-reliant in food and energy. He remarked:

> It would also mean the local people having more say in their own development and their own destiny than hitherto, and largely protect them from the vagaries of central decision makers, regional, national and international, far removed from their own personal situations, aspirations and frustrations.

Lewis admitted that his approach was "interventionist" and, in a modest way, technocratic. He pointed out, though, that his computer could test a mix of technologies in a few seconds, while to try it out in real life could mean twenty years of misdirected and miserable effort by the inhabitants of a village. The computer model gauged success by the proportion of the energy of daylight that was captured by the green pigments of plants growing by photosynthesis that was put to use by the villagers. Lewis also kept an eye on nutritional standards, care of the environment, and real-world economics. In contrast with piecemeal methods of accounting, the systems dynamics incorporated in the computer model gave a much clearer and often more hopeful picture of the gains achievable from particular innovations. Converted into rupees at the boundary between the village and the outside world, the figures showed whether or not the inhabitants could repay borrowed money quickly.

The research in Glasgow was instigated by the Swedish-based International Federation of Institutes for Advanced Study and done in collaboration with the Murugappa Chettiar Research Centre in Madras. In 1979–80 the scientists from Madras spent many months in the real Injambakkam, interviewing people and putting together detailed information about land use, agricultural methods and results, food and firewood, the availability of money, and so on. The profiles from these surveys enabled the researchers in Scotland to make sure that their computer simulation started true to life, and to set the electronic stage for a dramatic transformation of the village. The Indian scientists were testing a number of new technologies in local conditions at their Madras laboratory, and they earmarked Injambakkam as a place for introducing them to India's villagers. The role of the systems dynamics at Glasgow was to predict what would happen if a stipulated list of technologies entered service in a certain order over a period of years.

At the time of the survey Injambakkam was home for almost a thousand people. It occupied some 350 hectares (a hectare equals about 2.47 acres) of poor land, and the staple crop, rice, could be grown on only 56 hectares. There was firewood to be had, at the cost of much labor, from trees growing on the village land, but kerosene for lamps was brought in. Fewer than 24 hectares of rice paddy were under cultivation at any one time, because the villagers could not afford enough diesel fuel to pump water into the paddy, or enough fertilizer to put on it. Of their meager crop, 20 percent was eaten by pests after harvesting. As a result, even with two crops a year, the people were hungry, getting less than half the calories they needed, although fish from the nearby sea gave them some protection against protein malnutrition. One in five of all babies born in Injambakkam died before reaching the age of five.

More rice was the most urgent need, and the most obvious chance for biotechnological action lay at the feet of 200 cows and bullocks and 100 water buffaloes that roamed in Injambakkam and grazed on leaves and grass in waste plots in the village. Hindus could not eat their sacred cows, but there was nothing to stop them collecting the animals' dung and using it as manure or fuel. The Indian and British scientists set a high priority on installing a biogas plant, a tank where microbes could be set to work on the dung to produce a combustible gas consisting mainly of methane. The by-product would be a sludge rich in nitrogen in the form of urea and phosphorus in superphosphate and potassium phosphate—in short, an excellent fertilizer.

Biogas plants became a symbol of biotechnology's promise to the Third World. The Chinese led the way, installing millions of family-sized biogas plants, and the Indians were following behind. Community-sized plants were more economic than family units, but when the scientists visualized such a plant at Injambakkam they knew it would cost the equivalent of 10,000 U.S. dollars—a lot of money for very poor people. The biogas would run adapted diesel pumps to deliver irrigation water into the paddy. But would it really pay for itself?

Enter the systems dynamics expert, who could relate the products of the biogas plant to the potential yields of rice, as other innovations helped to boost output from the villagers' land. He could also test in his computer the likely effects of population growth, or emergencies such as drought or a failure of the biogas plant, and make sure that no catastrophe would follow. Development programs were tactfully adapted to what the villagers might be persuaded to do, step by step.

The aim was not to find the best system conceivable from a technological or economic point of view, but to schedule a sensible series of innovations, paced to suit the cautious villagers, that could alter the scenery and standards of living at Injambakkam in a radical manner. According to the program that evolved, the communal biogas plant was to go in first, in Year One. The villagers would earn the equivalent of a few U.S. cents per kilogram for delivering cow dung to the plant; later they could buy back sludge for fertilizing their fields.

Year Two was tree time, with the planting of 10 hectares (about 25 acres) of the fast-growing casuarina, or "she-oak." Other names of this tree told something about it: "beefwood" referred to the blood-brown color of the wood, "swamp oak," signified that it prospered in poor coastal soils, while the botanists' nomenclature, *Casuarina equisetifolia,* described its pendulous, horsetail-like foliage. None of these names disclosed why the she-oak was one of biotechnology's secret weapons for the tropics.

Besides being an excellent "energy tree," as a source of easily harvested firewood, the she-oak also produced its own fertilizer. Its roots harbored bacteria capable of fixing nitrogen from the air; its leaves could fertilize the fields for other crops. Ten hectares of she-oak should provide the better part of a ton (800 kilograms) of fixed nitrogen every year—enough to supply most of the nitrogen needed for an equal area of rice paddy.

Another tree with special properties was the neem or margosa (*Azadirachta indica*), a distant Burmese relative of the American poison ivy. The neem manufactured a potent insecticide in its seed kernels and leaves, and in Year Two of the Injambakkam program, the villagers were to start using locally produced neem extracts in preference to imported chemical pesticides. Complete substitution would take ten years to accomplish.

The chief event scheduled for Year Three was the introduction of a new variety of hybrid rice, Padma, offering a 14 percent improvement in the proportion of the rice protein that the human body could assimilate. At this time too, a five-year drive would begin, to replace the traditional cooking stoves of the villagers with wood-burning stoves of a more efficient design. To protect the harvested stocks of rice, the villagers would begin drying them better and storing them in containers out of reach of the jaws of rats and other pests.

By Year Four, the time would be ripe for inoculating the first of the rice paddy fields with free-living nitrogen-fixing bacteria. Rice farmers in large areas of India and Burma were already using combinations of various species of blue-green bacteria to cut their bills for chemical fertilizers by about 30 percent. At Injambakkam the inoculations were to take place over a period of four years. And in Year Five, the villagers would have a new crop.

Rice bean (*Vigna umbellata*), sneaked onto 10 hectares of Injambakkam's fields in the interval between the winter and summer rice crops, would supply humans with nourishing beans, and cows with abundant foliage. With nitrogen-fixing bacteria in nodules in its roots, the rice bean was to be yet another source of biological fertilization introduced into the system. That made four thus far: sludge from the biogas plant, the she-oak leaves, the blue-green inoculation, and the root nodules of the rice bean.

A fifth and potentially controversial source of nitrogen was to go on the fields starting in Year Six, when another large biogas plant would begin handling human excrement, and producing, like the cow-dung plant, fertilizing sludge as well as combustible gas. This second biogas plant would also accept 50 tons a year of water hyacinth, a weed to be harvested from the ponds and streams of Injambakkam, and would more than double the villagers' supply of gas.

The scenery at the village would change conspicuously in that same year (Year Six) when the first windmills, built of bamboo and jute to a modern design, began to take over some of the work of irrigating the fields. Over a period of five years or so, a hundred windmills would go up, and the chief benefit for the villagers would be the release of biogas to run two Fiat Totem engines that would produce electricity for lighting. In spite of being close to a major city, Injambakkam had no public electricity supply, so it would generate its own. By Year Seven, glimmers of electric light in the tropical darkness would tell a distant observer what the windmills proclaimed by day: that the village had pulled itself up by its bootstraps.

Excremental Apartheid

The numbers coming out of the computer in Glasgow looked beautiful. In seven years the villagers would be using the whole of their paddy for two crops a year, and would have more than three times as much food to eat as before. The inanimate energy assisting in food production would soar, while energy-saving practices, such as using waste heat from the electric generators to provide hot water, would help to make the villagers quite rich in fuel, in relation to their modest needs. They would be selling energy to other villages in the form of she-oak firewood.

Two key numbers confirmed the opportunity for advancement. Twelve years after the start, having paid off all their debts for buying equipment, the villagers would have the equivalent of about 4000 U.S. dollars in their communal bank account. And the capture of solar energy for human purposes would more than double, from 0.035 to 0.089 percent, bringing the efficiency of these poor Indian farmers to about one-tenth the level achieved on energy-intensive farms in Europe.

The systems dynamics revealed and built upon benefits left hidden by more simpleminded evaluations of the technologies. More energy and natural fertilizer meant better irrigation, bringing better nutrition for animals and people, which in turn led to more input for the biogas plants, and so on around a highly favorable feedback loop. To become essentially self-sufficient in food and energy, the villagers in the electronic Injambakkam ran their land, water supplies, and equipment as an integrated system for making the best possible use of the available sunlight. For them, reaching the promised land of self-reliance was a journey of only a few years.

It did not happen that way in the other Injambakkam. The development program implemented in reality by the biotechnologists of the Murugappa Chettiar Research Centre bore only a sketchy relationship to the plan hallmarked by the University of Strathclyde computer. The innovations were more haphazard, less carefully timetabled, and not nearly as well integrated as in the idealized scheme. The villagers were less conservative than expected about some innovations and more so about others. The biotechnologists were also beset by demands from other villages in the area that wanted the same treatment as Injambakkam. Professional enthusiasm and common humanity made these demands impossible to resist. That meant diluting the scientific effort at Injambakkam, and the project became less of a controlled experiment and more like a scrambled showcase.

By the mid-1980s, the visitor to Injambakkam would find windmills whirling ahead of schedule, she-oaks producing their firewood and fertilizer, and neems their pesticides. The water hyacinths and blue-greens were giving trouble, but extras not envisaged in the electronic scenario included a thriving system of biodynamic gardening: fish ponds enriched by duck droppings provided a source of fertile water and mud, which the villagers spread on new garden plots where they grew chilies, tomatoes, and watermelons. The people were plainly better off and better fed than they had been, although there were no objective data. The village had some biogas plants but they were small, family-sized units. The communal biogas plants, which promised energy self-sufficiency for the village as a whole, were still missing at the end of 1985—even the one intended to run on cattle dung.

India's ancient caste system was partly to blame—and not for the first time amid unfulfilled efforts to modernize the country. Brahmins and members of other castes had no wish to shovel the same cow shit as the Untouchables, who made up half the population of Injambakkam. The biotechnologists considered subdividing the biogas system, caste by caste, in an excremental "apartheid." The matter of biogas for Injambakkam illustrated a paradox at the core of strategies for self-reliance. On Monday you proclaimed the philosophy that development must meet the wishes and aspirations of the people involved, who were to learn to stand on their own feet economically and politically, and do things their way. On Tuesday, when you explained to them what you had in mind, they felt entitled to say, "We don't do things that way."

The upshot was that Chris Lewis's computer simulation of the imaginary Injambakkam remained a better guide to how the Third World villagers might arrive at a state of self-reliance in food and energy than anything to be seen along the shores of the Bay of Bengal. To be sure, local snags and loudmouthed objectors would crop up wherever innovations were proposed. But there were millions of villages, and some of them would see the point. This did not lie in any of the specific technologies in the idealized scenario, but in the collaborative systems approach that could multiply payoffs and astonish accountants.

Villages were no longer to be seen as collections of people, animals, fields, houses, and pieces of equipment dotted about on a large-scale map like a child's toy farmyard. They were green machines in which human beings and other organisms meshed with one another and with sunlight, air, water, and soil. Chemical compounds, most of them natural, were the fuel and working fluids of the machines.

The green machines were no technocratic fiction, nor a fanciful rendering of some facets of modern agriculture. The essence of life since the world began was the unconsciously concerted and self-regulated action of organisms sharing the same sunshine and trading the loose gases, liquids, and solids at the Earth's surface. Some of these natural green systems ran far more productively than others, and there were always unrealized opportunities. The two-legged animals with clever brains, a capacity for concerted action, and a will to self-reliance had plenty to play for in rearranging parts of the systems.

In India's capital, New Delhi, the National Biotechnology Board promulgated in 1983 its plan for mobilizing the country's scientists to achieve national self-sufficiency in food, clothing, and housing, combined with "appropriate" industrial growth and the creation of new jobs. Immediate objectives included more efficient production of bioethanol (alcohol) from molasses; in the long run the aim was to use materials from living plants to create protein and fats for eating, fuel for burning, and chemicals for manufacture, so as to establish a decentralized industrial base.

New Delhi itself was the designated site for one of two laboratories of the International Centre of Genetic Engineering and Biotechnology, created by twenty-six nations. It was charged with research in agriculture and health relevant to Third World needs. The fixing of nitrogen by biological means, and the resistance of plants to drought loomed large in the research program. The other laboratory, at Trieste, Italy, was expected to concentrate on industrial methods, looking for biological means of manufacturing useful products from plants, and developing industrial-scale methods of fermentation. The twin laboratories were symptomatic of the new enthusiasm for biotechnology that was sweeping the world in the 1980s.

If villagers in the Third World could aspire to self-reliance by biotechnology, why not the rest of the human species? The richer people were, the more thoroughly they seemed to be emmeshed in global spiders' webs of food, energy, and manufacture. They ran Japanese-built cars on Arabian fuel, and drank Brazilian coffee, Indian tea, and the juice of California oranges. If they wanted to stay rich they could not, at first sight, ever expect to take charge of their own destinies, but must remain forever subject, in Chris Lewis's words, to "the vagaries of central decision makers, regional, national and international." So high interest rates in New York threw European craftsmen into terminal unemployment. Towns were created or destroyed by the whims of multinational companies deciding where to locate their operations. About five individuals in the world had the personal authority to unleash nuclear war, and the targets were mostly in the richer countries. Politically their inhabitants seemed to be in far worse case than the Indian peasants, when it came to running their own lives.

Yet the biotechnologies that already offered self-reliance in the Third World were rudimentary. The Madras-Glasgow prospectus for the Coromandel Coast made no mention of genetic engineering to produce meatier rice; nor was there any idea of manufacturing plastic sheets from the water hyacinths, or growing jute fiber for the windmill sails in glass bottles. Microcomputers were ideal for monitoring the performance of a biodynamic system day by day, but these were not envisaged for Injambakkam.

More complex needs (or demands) of the inhabitants of the richer countries could be met by more complex biotechnologies, to which they had easier access and which they could better afford. Glasgow, Göttingen, and Grand Rapids shared the sunlight and air with Injambakkam, and there was no reason in principle why they should not aspire to self-reliance, too, by shrewd use of green machinery.

On the other side of this high-technology coin was a promise that the Third World villagers, too, could hope for much higher living standards, without destroying their environment or abandoning newly won self-reliance and political self-confidence. Even the well-fed villagers of Lewis's idealized scenario had only a few dollars a head in their communal bank account after twelve years' labor. To reach different orders of magnitude of communal wealth, whether measured in cash or in facilities such as housing, transport, education, and medical care, would require biotechnology of more advanced kinds.

Biotechnology and the Green Machines

People made "biotechnology" mean whatever they wanted, as the focus of technical and commercial interest shifted. In the 1970s it usually referred to modern analogs of brewing and cheese making: the use by the chemical industry of microorganisms and enzymes, the natural promoters of chemical reactions. Agriculture was sometimes specifically counted out. In 1980 all of Wall Street knew that biotechnology meant genetic engineering for medical purposes, and investors rushed to buy shares in biotechnology companies of that inclination. By 1985, people were speaking of the "new biotechnology," and the semantic telescope was swinging from the hospitals toward the farms.

The Commission of the European Communities in Brussels had designated, as the new biotechnology, the applied biological science "which is relevant to the removal of current scientific and technical barriers to the promotion of health and the development of industry and agriculture." This being such a catchall, the commission felt bound to give examples of what it had in mind: enzyme technology; genetic engineering to produce new living entities; molecular biology in medical diagnostics and vaccine manufacture; the culture of microorganisms, animal cells, and plant cells; the regeneration of plants from plant cells; and the manufacture of useful materials from plant and animal products not needed as food.

A pragmatic definition held that anyone who claimed to be a biotechnologist probably was, and biotechnology was whatever biotechnologists did when they were working. In agriculture and industry their work was the conception of new green machines. The color was not to be taken too literally. As the physicist Freeman Dyson put it, "Factories are gray, gardens are green. Physics is gray, biology is green. Plutonium is gray, horse manure is green . . ."

"Green" for ecological activists signaled concern for the human relationship with living nature. The present author set "machines" behind it in deliberate oxymoron—a figure of speech like "bittersweet." It denoted metaphorically the interaction of parts in a system, but also conveyed a certain technical and political tough-mindedness; the plural implied pluralism. At definition time, "green machines" meant engineered systems using biological and biochemical processes or their manmade analogs, to create food, materials, energy, or other goods and services.

The engineering included equipment such as greenhouses or fermentation tanks, and techniques like artificial seed making or genetic engineering, but it was concerned also with the overall design of systems, including their social and economic aspects. There were no obligatory or limiting rules, but green was cool. Green machines typically eschewed the high temperatures associated with gray machines and their power plants, except when they used the 5500°C surface of the sun as source of high-grade energy.

Although "green" expressed a bias toward chlorophyll and that natural green pigment's role in trapping particles of daylight, the interchangeability of different forms of energy—light, heat, electricity, energy of movement, chemical energy—multiplied the options for designers. For example, a green machine might grow plants using electric light generated by water power or nuclear power. The bulk of the throughput would normally consist of organic (carbon-based) materials such as sugars and proteins, largely constructed from water and the carbon dioxide and nitrogen of the air. The jargon word for such materials was "biomass": flour and flesh were biomass, and so were straw and bones. An endless confusion for English speakers was the use of the word "plant" for either a vegetable organism or a factory. Biotechnological processing plants could operate on the biomass produced by biotechnologically engineered living plants.

Green machines transformed organic materials by natural or artificial means. For example, the most popular green machines of 1980, the biogas plants, used microorganisms to turn organic wastes into combustible methane gas, which was also known as marsh gas because Nature produced it in boggy terrain. Cows, humans, and other animals farted methane. In fact Nature's own methane industry supplied an important component of the chemical traffic of the Earth's atmosphere, with some microbes making it and others busily removing it. Rural communities in China and India hijacked a piece of this system for their own use.

A biogas plant was a vat made of bricks, concrete, steel, or rigid plastic, usually buried to keep it warm, which had a bell, bag or tube on top to collect the gas. If the input was manure, it was diluted with an equal volume of water. Designers and operators had to be sure of keeping out the air because the team of naturally occurring microorganisms that did the work hated oxygen. Some of them broke down large molecules into small ones, from which others made carbon dioxide and hydrogen. Acetic acid was a by-product that also acted as an inhibitor, so adding lime to neutralize it speeded the fermentation. Finally the microscopic methane makers took the carbon dioxide and replaced the oxygen atoms by hydrogen atoms. The processes required about two weeks at a temperature somewhat above body heat, and during that time most disease-causing organisms in the manure were killed off. None of the processes went to completion: About half of the original material remained as an undigested sludge, and the biogas contained 30 to 40 percent unconverted carbon dioxide, along with other impurities. Even so, the biogas from a liter of organic waste could match, in the best circumstances, the energy content of nearly half a liter of gasoline.

More elaborate concepts for green machines appeared in a Japanese artist's impression of a rural scene, shown to visitors in Tokyo by Masashi Kobayashi, a research counsellor at the Ministry of Agriculture, Forestry and Fisheries. The picture looked like an ordinary farming community, complete with cows and logging operations, but with additions. It was a game of "spot the technology." Some items were large-scale equivalents of those at Injambakkam: a big biogas plant, for example, and a pond growing water hyacinths and fertilizing bacteria. To these were added energy-saving greenhouses, and retorts for turning husks and straw into combustible gas, by heat. One field carried sweet sorghum, the fastest-growing "energy crop" for Japanese conditions. With the help of mushrooms, a biochemical plant turned wood from fast-growing trees into sugar. In the nearby sea, floating frames carried cultivated seaweed, which went for processing in a factory on the shore.

The picture showed technologies that were already available to any rural communities that cared to put them together. The Japanese were short of farmland in relation to the size of their population, but that was an incentive for them to make the best use of what little they had. Kobayashi was helping to plan the fifteen-year, 200-million-dollar research effort in biotechnology for agriculture that his ministry was just launching. One of its aims was to encourage the adoption of existing technologies, but the Japanese would have to be weaned from their love of mass production. Akihiko Hayami, a research coordinator at the ministry, declared, "Biomass resources spread thin and in vast areas should be utilized locally on a small-scale basis."

The main effort of the Japanese agrobiotechnology program was in plant breeding, using the latest techniques in cell culture and genetic engineering to help develop, for example, cold-resistant strains of rice for Japan's northeast provinces, and more nutritious cereal crops. New varieties of frost-resistant potatoes and sweet potatoes would be introduced to the farmers. Japanese scientists were also monitoring the efforts of genetic engineers in Europe and the United States to develop cereal crops capable of fixing their own nitrogen from the air; their own preliminary verdict was "difficult."

An ambitious aim of Japanese molecular geneticists was to make water-resistant wheat and soybeans that could grow in paddy fields like those used for rice. Researchers at Tsukuba, the science city near Tokyo, identified a gene that conferred water resistance on barley, and which might be transferred to other crops. An early effort in the agriculture ministry's new program would be to develop a gene bank at Tsukuba so as to preserve alive 200,000 natural varieties of plants akin to the species of crops of interest to Japan.

At Tsukuba's Expo '85 visitors waited patiently in line to see a far-out Japanese image of the green machines of the twenty-first century. The lines were not as long as those for the Fuyo robot theater and its apotheosis of the gray machines, but people who penetrated the green dome of the Midori-Kan pavilion heard the genetic code by DNA set to music. "Biotechnology Opens the New Century" was the proclamation.

A multiscreen cartoon movie took the audience to a distant planet, green and fertile, where the people of an advanced civilization lived in skyscrapers shaped like twirls of meringue. The inhabitants of Bio strolled in the city's biotechnical park and admired the enzymes at work making valuable materials. A structure like the Sydney Opera House painted green turned out to be the gene bank that guarded the genetic inheritance of the planet. An abundance of rocket ships and "biochips"— electronic devices using biomolecules—denoted the planet's affluence. The commentary finished in the Japanese way by instructing the visitors to work to make the promise of biotechnology come true on Earth.

For all the artistic imagination that went into it, the image of the planet Bio at Tsukuba was curiously austere. The people wore uniform jump suits. The lush landscapes around the city looked like farmland and parkland groomed to human needs and tastes, rather than places where wild animals and plants might continue an existence outside the gene bank. Instead of rural green machines of the kind visualized by Hayami, Bio seemed to possess large-scale industries. There was no hint of any social order that might strike a Japanese visitor as unusual.

Alternative visions for a planet of green machines were possible. In a "soft" version, offered by the present author in the 1960s, a million villages or microcities would be scattered like ships in a deliberately created wilderness where nonhuman species could prosper. The inhabitants of the villages would use their technology to pursue two contradictory aims. They would obtain their food and as many other products as possible from sunlight, air, and water, and at the same time reduce their demands on the land. In shorthand, the objectives would be: (1) to implode agriculture; (2) to miniaturize cities for social and aesthetic reasons; and (3) to embark on an "environment game" aimed at restoring and extending the diversity of animals and plants on the Earth. An ecologically wild planet was a primary objective.

In a "hard" version, better suited to altered aspirations twenty years later, the scenery of the greened planet might finish up looking very much the same, but that would be a long-term consequence of devolution undertaken to tame the wild beasts of politics and economics. An entirely different set of purposes and priorities would be at work. Again in shorthand: (1) to defend rural communities against dissolution by agribusinesses; (2) to evacuate the cities before they were destroyed by nuclear bombs; (3) to secure as many people as possible against the consequences of nuclear winter. In the Third World, people would be striving for those things; also (4) to adapt to the destruction of export markets by biotechnology; and (5) to leapfrog over the gray-machine phase of northern industrial history and achieve prosperity by means of rural green machines. For country-dwellers everywhere, the primary objective would become (6) to dissolve the nation-states.

The condition of the world in the late twentieth century made the strongly politicized ("hard") route toward a green Earth more plausible than the "soft" way. The prospect of poverty, dispossession, or annihilation was more likely to spur people to action than any amount of rhetoric about environmental or aesthetic concerns. The latter were indeed fundamental for the biological and mental health of human societies, and would have to be heeded at every stage. But in the end the hopes of environmentalists might be fulfilled more generously by the "hard" route, once the political ground was literally cleared and high biotechnology had created green machines of dazzling efficiency.

The Price of Plenty

Conventional farms were two-dimensional chemical factories, and for anyone with a true feeling for life nothing was more irritating than to hear a city dweller commenting on a pastoral scene: "Isn't Nature wonderful." Farms and ranches were always highly unnatural enterprises. In the twentieth century people became more aware of this, when they saw tractors hauling inorganic fertilizers and light aircraft spraying chemical pesticides and herbicides on the crops. Yet these were just modern variations on a much older and more profound artificiality. The assaults on Nature's ways began in the worst of the most recent ice age, when people in the Levant started herding gazelles and goats instead of hunting them, and others in the Nile Valley made tentative experiments in sowing barley and wheat.

After the ice age, horticulturalists equipped with different packages of crops and domesticated animals radiated from independent centers in Indochina, Indonesia, southwestern Asia, the African Sahel, and Middle America, gradually taking over ever-larger tracts of the most fertile lands and dispossessing their wildlife and the human hunters. Civil engineering began with prehistoric irrigation schemes—early green machines that made dry land unnaturally fertile. Large-scale drainage extended the cultivable areas even into the swampy forests of Middle America. The farmers were not conscious chemists, but they labored to make the daylight produce edible protein and starch of preselected kinds. They felled forests, attacked the soil with hoes, and let their fields sprawl extravagantly across the countryside to capture as much sunlight as possible.

The hunger for land continued for 10,000 years, and peaked in the mid-twentieth century. A surge in human numbers began in China around 1700, spread to Europe a century later, and became global by 1930. To feed the soaring populations farmers cleared more forests, drained more swamps, extended their irrigation schemes, and put unsuitable hillsides under the plow. The human species worked feverishly at this task, spurred on by predictions of certain famine. Between 1945 and 1960 the area of land under cultivation in the world grew by 50 percent.

Around 1960 another equally amazing transition occurred. Although the population boom was still accelerating, the rate at which new land came into cultivation slowed down dramatically. Yet food production continued to increase significantly faster than the world's population grew. A revolution in farming pushed up the yields from each hectare. It involved huge increases in the proportion of irrigated land and in the use of artificial fertilizers. It also included the magic seeds of new varieties of wheat and rice for the Third World's "green revolution."

Agricultural technology was paying off handsomely, and the

American plant breeder Norman Borlaug won the 1970 Nobel Peace Prize for his work in Mexico that created the "miraculous" semi-dwarf wheats. The chemical industry, though, could claim much of the credit. By 1985, as Lester Brown of the Worldwatch Institute expressed it, the additional food produced with chemical fertilizer was feeding a billion and a half people. In other words, without industrial chemistry one person in three should be dead.

In India, which had been a food beggar in the early 1960s, wheat production increased nearly fivefold in twenty years, from 10 million tons in 1964 to 46 million tons in 1985. Rice production in Indonesia trebled in the same interval, and agronomists had similar success stories to relate from China and other densely populated countries of Asia. Population growth rates were easing, and the prophets of global famine were confounded.

Events were at least as remarkable in the rich countries. The yields per hectare of corn (maize) in the United States doubled between 1960 and 1975. The areas of land under cultivation shrank, and the number of farm workers diminished. For example, 13 percent of France's cropland went out of production between 1960 and 1980, and the labor force dropped by 56 percent, while the country's output of food went on increasing.

Science had helped to cause the global population explosion by its application in tropical medicine; science was now coping with the consequences by producing abundant food. Sub-Saharan Africa was the crisis spot, where repeated years of drought brought starvation and death to many people. The species that could send men to the moon and robot spacecraft to Uranus and Halley's comet was feckless about shifting grain quickly to remote parts of the African Sahel. Despite the best rains for a decade, in 1985, UN officials declared that 25 million people were still at risk, and predicted that the situation in Africa would get worse before it could get better. Food production per head of the rapidly growing population was declining, and although aid in the form of money and food was only a stopgap it would be needed for some years to come. Once-fertile land was turning to desert in a deadly interplay of climate and human pressure on the soil. The way to drive back the desert would be by irrigation, but that would require general economic advancement in the afflicted countries.

Plant breeders hoped to develop varieties of wheat and other cereals better able to withstand drought, but some thought more attention should be paid to indigenous African grain crops better adapted to poor soils and unreliable rainfall. For example, the t'ef of Ethiopia, which made a flat bread called *injera*, was almost as high-yielding as wheat, even though far less scientific breeding effort had gone into it. A complication was that Africans had recently acquired a taste for wheat bread, which owed its baking qualities to cross-links between protein molecules created in the kneading process. Genetic engineers could try to introduce similar proteins into the flour of African millet and sorghum, so as to produce a better bread.

Even in countries where food production soared, the picture was marred. The poorest farmers of the Third World lost out if they could not afford to irrigate their land or buy fertilizer to make proper use of the magic seeds. Soil erosion, catastrophic in a few places and creeping insidiously in many others, seemed likely to increase demands for expensive fertilizer. Some 300 million people remained undernourished or malnourished, and unpredictable bad weather could cut yields at any time. So could plant diseases, and the huge areas planted monoculturally with the same high-yielding varieties of plants were especially prone to attack.

Overproduction was nevertheless hair-raising for many farmers. The efforts to feed the world had overshot the mark, not in terms of satisfying human needs everywhere, but in what the markets could handle. Even with large grain-producing areas of North America idled (deliberately put out of production) the world produced a record 1.9 billion tons of grain in 1985. The carry-over of unconsumed grain at the end of the 1985–86 season was estimated at more than 300 million tons, and world trade in cereals was declining. Between 1981 and 1986 the international price of wheat dropped by more than one-third.

In the United States, land prices in the corn belt, which had quadrupled during the 1970s, began to fall in the 1980s.

Farmers' incomes were slashed. Many of those who were not driven out of farming strove for greater self-sufficiency—for example by using less fertilizer and pesticides, or by saving straw for use in animal feed and as a source of energy. Conservationists approved, but the result was a deliberate reduction in yields per acre. The big commercial farms continued to chase the yields upward.

The family farm loomed large in American folklore and ideology. In the newborn United States, when Thomas Jefferson the decentralizer wrangled with Alexander Hamilton the nationalist, Jefferson saw independent farmers as guardians of democracy and key figures in the diffusion of political power to the people. The reality of the 1980s was that one-third of the cropland and two-thirds of the net income in American farming went to 1 percent of the farms, run as commercial enterprises. Beef cattle and broiler chickens were largely in the hands of a small number of very large producers, as agriculture rapidly concentrated in the manner of other industries, with the largest feed manufacturers raising their own animals. The rise of large agribusiness operators, independent of the local communities, led to the decline or disappearance of small rural towns and their social institutions. The Office of Technology Assessment of the U.S. Congress reported that the rural communities in California dominated by large integrated farms had fewer services, poorer education, and less community spirit.

Natural communities were also threatened. Environmentalists were dismayed by the frequent indifference of agribusiness to local ecosystems. Streams became polluted by the chemicals strewn on the fields and into the air. The enlargement of farms and fields, driven by extraneous economics, often required the destruction of many hedgerows and coppices that harbored birds, insects, and other animals. Agricultural methods were perceived as a worse threat to the environment than the activities of the energy and manufacturing industries.

Small might be beautiful, but very small was not. Luther Tweeten of Oklahoma State University, in a review (1983) of social and technical studies of real life on American farms, showed that many sentimental beliefs about small farms were the opposite of the truth. People on farms grossing less than $40,000 a year felt demoralized and alienated. Soil erosion was worse on small farms, and their energy inputs were higher in relation to yields. Tweeten's optimum was a farm of a moderate size, grossing about $100,000 a year, which was large enough to achieve economies of scale and low prices for most farm produce, yet not so large as to lose the personal touch.

Biotechnology would help to safeguard both the human and the ecological communities. New rural industries using green machines could stanch the loss of people and wealth from the communities. The genetic engineers' quest for quasi-natural systems for fertilizing crops seemed a better bet than either a continued massive use of costly synthetic fertilizers or a regression to medieval, low-yield agriculture. Even existing technologies had plenty to offer, when environmental factors were put into the balance.

A biogas plant might seem unattractive and a needless expense to farmers in North America or Western Europe, with plenty of energy to be had from other sources, until they and their neighbors took into account the terrible smell that came from pigsties, and the cost of disposing of the manure in a nonpolluting fashion. Runoffs of waste from animal houses killed fish in streams and released into the environment microorganisms that caused disease in human beings, livestock, and wild animals. Seen in a systems perspective, biogas plants made sense, and experiments in Scotland showed that pig manure fermented into methane at an exceptionally high rate. The Commissariat Français à l'Énergie Solaire began encouraging people in French rural areas to install biogas plants, reminding them that many of their grandfathers had used them successfully during the German occupation of 1940–44.

Institutionalized Glut

Pig manure was a potent weapon of civil protest when dumped from a tanker truck onto a city bridge, as the farmers of Brittany well knew, especially if the wind was right for wafting the stench toward the offices of those with whom the country dwellers were in dispute. Tractors could jam the traffic of cities, and the authorities in Paris and Washington were dismayed when militant farmers thronged the streets with their lumbering vehicles. The farmers had more political muscle in rich countries, where they made up a very small part of the population, than in poor countries where they outnumbered the city dwellers yet had little say in their policies.

Farmers always grumbled, and not without reason. Bad weather hit their harvests and their profits. Perfect weather, on the other hand, resulted in gluts of food that sent free-market prices plummeting, and again cut the farmers' profits, perhaps forcing them to destroy unmarketable crops. Agricultural science and technology pushed up yields in North America and Europe until overproduction became normal. By effective organization, lobbying, and making the most of the political geography that gave them control of crucial constituencies, the farmers of North America and Western Europe were able to institutionalize the glut. Their fellow citizens paid twice over: in taxes for multi-billion-dollar subsidies to the farmers, and high food prices in the shops. For farmers in the rich countries, the law of supply and demand was repealed.

The reward for the taxpayers was a prosperous countryside that made their regions largely self-sufficient in food production. This was not a bad objective, even though the price was high. Paying extra for self-sufficiency was an old concept, whether it was a matter of subsidies or of tariffs, quotas, and contraband regulations against imports. The motives might be fiscal, social, or military, but the upshot was that goods seldom changed hands at the rock-bottom world price. And the most spectacular results were evident in the countries of the European Economic Community (Common Market). Despite their hearty appetites, the Europeans achieved self-sufficiency in most foodstuffs and went on to produce surpluses on a gargantuan scale.

Mountains of grain, sugar, and butter, Saharas of dried milk, and lakes of wine and olive oil grew at an embarrassing rate. As it cost, for example, 40 cents to preserve a kilogram of butter for a year, huge storage bills were added to the farming subsidies that helped to create the surpluses. More than half of Britain's grain harvest of 1985 went straight into the stockpiles. The standard prices were far too high for getting rid of the surpluses on the world market, but butter sold off to the Soviet Union at a knockdown price enabled the Russians to spend more on guns.

The material fact was that the intensively farmed fields of Europe reliably produced very rich harvests. They did so with the help of large inputs of inanimate energy in the form of fertilizers and machinery. Nevertheless the open fields beneath Europe's gray skies were the most productive in history, and they turned solar energy into produce with an efficiency of conversion on the order of 1 percent.

A grand question confronted Europe's agronomists, industrialists, and politicians as they brought their minds into focus about biotechnology. Could the farmers be kept in business and their surpluses put to good use by using agriculture as the basis of new industries? Plant starch, for example, traditionally starched shirts and paper and made sizings and glue; biological and chemical processing could transform it into an unlimited range of organic chemicals, from plastics in bulk to high-priced pharmaceutical products. With world prices of starch falling rapidly, in relation to the price of oil, it was already cheaper than the ethylene used as a key feedstock by the chemical industry.

The Vice-President of the Commission of the European Communities, Karl-Heinz Narjes, declared in November 1985:

> The biological revolution must lead to agro-industrial transformation. . . . We can begin to develop new crop plants, and better harvesting, separation, and processing techniques, thus reducing costs and opening up new markets. We can redirect agriculture towards an expanding and sustainable future. . . . We must invest in science, not in surpluses.

When Narjes said this, citric acid factories were closing because of the high cost of starch within the EEC, while starch was exported at subsidized prices to industrial competitors in non-EEC countries. Although Narjes painted an optimistic picture of the technological opportunities, especially concerning new crops for Europe and their "fractionation" into multiple uses, he could not evade the central political issue. The prices of potential biological feedstocks for industry, notably starch and sugar, were much higher in Europe than in the world markets, because they were governed by the support prices of the Common Agricultural Policy. This meant that manufacturers of biotechnological products would base their operations elsewhere, and Europe would have to import the products.

Drastic reductions in the prices for starch and sugar for nonfood uses were proposed by the European Commission to the Council of Ministers, the top body in the EEC, so that industries within Europe could buy them at prices comparable with those in other parts of the world. Politicians spotted at once that the special pricing could amount to an extension of the subsidies paid by European taxpayers, this time to the industrialists. The European Council of Chemical Manufacturers Federations observed sourly that the proposed cut of 32.5 percent in the European price of sugar for industrial use would still leave them paying twice the world price.

Europe's political machinery, which required unanimity among governments for any change in policy, seemed unlikely to produce a quick shift from surpluses to science. The long-term aim would have to be to increase the farmers' income while lowering food prices and without grossly expanding production. The answer to this riddle was for biotechnology to make the nonfood components of the crop plants a major source of income for the farmers.

Agricultural Refineries

Danish biotechnologists were the most vocal in Europe in proclaiming the scientific opportunities. Big ideas from a small country were not really surprising. Novo Industri in Bagsvaerd led the world in the production of enzymes used in the food and washing-powder industries, and Denmark's most famous brewery had long been a generous sponsor of scientific research.

The aim of decentralizing industrial operations to the rural communities was uppermost in the mind of Lars Munck of the Carlsberg Research Foundation. Slashing transport costs was one motive; another was the creation of jobs for people put out of work by the automation of farming. Munck described in a proposal for Eureka (a cooperative technology program for Western Europe) how he would like to fit out the local farmer with an "individualized" computer-controlled production system. This would extend from remote sensors in the growing areas to up-to-the-minute guidance on the state of the market.

A local "agricultural refinery" would be the chief instrument by which small farmers could benefit from growth of biotechnological industry. As Munck explained the concept to members of the European Parliament at hearings on biotechnology late in 1985, the agricultural refinery would take in the whole crop—grain, straw, leaves, and all—and pretreat it for many uses. Some of the grain would go to the elevators for marketing as food, but some would be sent to a starch plant for use in chemical manufacturing. Protein returned from the starch plant to the agricultural refinery would make animal feed when mixed with other local material—treated straw, leaf material, and grain. Straw would go to a pulp mill for the cellulose industry, or else to a board-making plant.

Munck had in mind some continent-wide objectives for the European Economic Community, to cut grain surpluses on the one hand and agricultural imports on the other. Straw would replace some of the wood fiber imported by EEC countries for making paper and board. And high-yielding varieties of rape, sunflower, soybean and similar crops, introduced onto European farms, could reduce the Community's need to buy in edible oils, and proteins for animal feed. Munck visualized the agricultural refinery dispatching the produce to an oil-extraction plant, which would again return protein for the local feed mill.

The use of the grain itself as a raw material for the chemical industry was the boldest element in Munck's scheme. The forecasts indicated that by A.D. 2000 the EEC could be producing grain surpluses of around 60 million tons a year. Switching more of these to animal feed might reduce the total, but improvements in farm productivity might equally increase them. If the price were right, surpluses could in principle replace imported petroleum as a feedstock for making industrial chemicals and plastics.

These proposals did not spring unbidden from a Danish group working in isolation from other Europeans. Lars Munck and his Carlsberg colleague Finn Rexen first formulated their ideas in a report to the Commission of the European Communities in Brussels. That was in the course of a sustained effort by which the commission had, since 1978, sought to foster European interest and cooperation in biotechnology, under the acronyms FAST and CUBE.

A marriage between advanced agricultural techniques and biotechnological industries would give birth to a new kind of "bio-society," according to the authors of the FAST study. The aim would be to obtain from each hectare of Europe's farmland the maximum sustainable "added value" and employment opportunities. In 1984 the "bio-society" subgroup of FAST (Forecasting and Assessment in Science and Technology) was reincarnated as CUBE (Concertation Unit for Biotechnology in Europe). A Biomolecular Engineering Programme began disbursing more than a hundred research contracts to promote collaborative progress in enzyme engineering and genetic engineering. These encouraged advances in cloning vaccines for farm animals, in cloning genes involved in cheese making and the digestion of wood, in designing advanced chemical reactors to run on enzymes, and in identifying plant genes of high commercial value.

CUBE monitored the EEC's member states' own efforts in biotechnology. It also kept reminding everyone of the problems of safety, and also the difficulties that biotechnology in industrialized countries could cause for the Third World. With steadily mounting support at the highest levels of the commission, the CUBE team spelled out the needs for Europe-wide action in language that became increasingly pointed and political. To the relatively bland proposals for demonstration projects, research networks, and training schemes were added sharp criticisms of Europe's educational capacity in biology, and of the EEC's sacred cow, the Common Agricultural Policy.

There were differences of opinion within the commission. The agricultural directorate visualized surplus land going out of production and the countryside becoming increasingly a park for tourism and recreation. Continuing high subsidies for a dwindling number of farmers would make them, in effect, highly paid gardeners and gamekeepers for urban man's rural estates. The vision was congenial for many "back-to-Nature" activists in Europe, and Friends of the Earth condemned any idea of turning grain into chemical products as "an industrial assault on the biosphere." But such attitudes also matched uncomfortably well the Japanese predictions that Europe was to become the world's museum, living off tourists rather than industrial products.

The science and technology directorate insisted that surplus land could be used more creatively to develop manufacturing industry based on agriculture. Ken Sargeant of the CUBE team told a meeting in Cambridge, England, in 1985, that Europe had some big advantages:

> It has much more land than the Japanese, with a steady supply becoming available for new uses. It has a strong agricultural base, thanks to a successful agricultural policy that has encouraged the achievement of the highest yields of grain per hectare of any in the world. It has a powerful chemical industry, bigger than those of the United States and Japan, that is strongly innovative in the biological field, holding, for example, three-quarters of the world market in industrial enzymes. It has a strong and innovative pharmaceutical industry. These industrial strengths rest on an equally powerful and diverse pure and applied research base in the natural sciences that has produced many of the world's recent Nobel prize winners in these fields.

Pluralistic Europe would not find it easy to get its act together. Sargeant's colleague Mark Cantley recalled Cassandra, the Trojan princess whom Apollo blessed with the gift of prophecy and cursed with the rider that she would never be believed. "The greatest difficulty," Cantley observed, "is neither in forecasting strategic change, nor in identifying what needs to be done, but in communicating these messages to a structure impervious to receiving and maladapted to acting upon such messages." In Cantley's view, Europeans faced a philosophical question: whether to try to work coherently and purposefully together, with a continent-wide and indeed global outlook, or to cling to their traditions of the "open society" and "piecemeal [social] engineering" as commended by the philosopher Karl Popper. CUBE, like the EEC in general, was dedicated to purposeful action, but the responses of Europe's nations were often minimal, except in reaction to external threats of a medical or military nature. Early meetings of minds in biotechnology occurred much more readily among scientists and technologists scattered across Europe, than among the governments. To the outside observer, it looked as if CUBE ought to deliver its messages directly to Europe's rural populations.

For anyone interested in the future shape of the world, the long-winded discussions about biotechnology among European politicians, bureaucrats, industrialists, and scientists were fascinating precisely because they were long-winded. They were unmatched anywhere else, and never before in the history of technology had there been such wide-ranging debate in anticipation of innovations. The Japanese and Americans trusted their industrial entrepreneurs to seize the technological opportunities and run with them. This was a well-proven route to fast innovation and commercial success, so Europeans had good reason to fear being left behind.

In the U.S. and Japan the profit motive in the chemical companies, rather than concern about lifestyles and political control, was likely to set the course for the biotechnological revolution. The chances were it would continue the bad habits of the earlier industrial revolution, especially those of bullying corporations indifferent about places and ready to treat people as expendable tools. If the traditional farmer was obsolete, he could be swept aside by the green machines, just as rural craftsmen were overwhelmed by the gray machines of the nineteenth century. Farming areas might very well degenerate into solar-energy collectors for big industries—reminiscent of the quasi-colonial plantations in the Third World, but worked by robots rather than people.

With European companies daunted by high agricultural

prices and awaiting help from the politicians, the help could be made conditional on protecting people of the countryside and their ways of life. The best assurance of such an outcome was the conservative stubbornness of the farmers, in an unexpected alliance with Europe's democratic-socialist tradition that people and their communities and environments mattered more than the profit motive. For capitalist entrepreneurs, rural sentimentality and softhearted socialism were the two lamest legs of the European tortoise. Yet at the end of the race the American and Japanese hares might find themselves with a depopulated and dispirited countryside, while Europeans patiently adapted the technology to suit the villagers and reaped the benefits of coherent systems.

The political and cultural pluralism of Europe made it virtually certain that, somewhere on the continent, imaginative and determined rural communities would pioneer the development of high-tech villages. Self-reliant development from the bottom up remained an option for Europeans as well as for the farmers of the Third World. In the absence of an agreed EEC policy for raw-material prices, technologically minded farmers could circumvent the Community by taking the materials from their fields and putting them straight into their own fermentation tanks, with no money changing hands until there were chemical products for sale. EEC regulations in the mid-1980s favored the farmer over the industrialist.

The quirks of agropolitical history thus made some Western Europeans eager to disperse agricultural biotechnology across the countryside. The motive was to keep Europe's well-paid farmers in the style of life to which they were accustomed, as inexpensively as possible, by maximizing the farmers' returns from the new biotechnological industries and creating new jobs for those displaced by automated crop production. The Common Agricultural Policy, which caused the intense financial pressures, was tailored to appease the small peasant farmers of France, Italy, and other agriculturally conservative countries. The upshot was that Europe's peasants, pampered by taxpayers and technologists, were in a strong position to start leading the world into an era of decentralized green machines.

Diesel Trees and Gasoline Ponds

Should petroleum be used for producing food, or should food be converted into fuel to replace petroleum? This conundrum, at the dawn of the new era of green machines, revealed a high degree of flexibility in the chemical and biological processes. There was nevertheless irony in the chemical industries' manufacture of protein by cultivating microorganisms on their fuels or chemical products while other industrialists were busily turning sugar and other crops into fuels.

As agriculture was becoming more efficient, the price of oil was rising. In the late 1960s, a ton of maize (corn) cost as much as 5.5 tons of oil, but by the 1980s maize was cheaper than oil. Could this change in relative prices trigger an industrial revolution? Some people thought so, and more radical than the use of crops to replace petroleum as a feedstock for the chemical industry would be the replacement of petroleum as a fuel.

The tyranny of world prices was, though, an impediment to clear thinking. Oil reserves were not unlimited, and this was reflected in the great price rises of the 1970s. But the reserves of suitable land for growing "energy crops" were not unlimited either, a fact sometimes forgotten by enthusiasts anxious to go green at every opportunity. A fall in oil prices in 1986 was discouraging for promoters of all forms of alternative energy. Nevertheless, the idea of growing liquid fuels was popular, not least because certain plants cried out to be used for this purpose.

The Franco-German inventor of the diesel engine had been a green technologist ahead of his time. After he developed his spark-free internal combustion engine in the 1890s, Rudolf Diesel became briefly a millionaire. But he was also an enemy of national governments, a pacifist, and an advocate of labor reform and global justice, who wanted his engines to provide mechanical power for all the world's small manufacturers. To this end, the engines should be extremely versatile in respect to fuel, and able to run on low-grade petroleum, powdered coal, combustible gas, rancid butter, or palm oil.

In the end, the diesel engine was perfected to run on a particular fraction of distilled petroleum, heavier than gasoline, and with that fuel it drove many of the world's ships, buses, trucks, trains, and tractors. But farmers temporarily out of the standard fuel found that their diesel engines would run on vegetable oils. As worries mounted about petroleum—its high price and its eventual exhaustion—engineers remembered Diesel's dream, and tested vegetable oils more systematically in the hope of giving a new meaning to "flower power."

The results were encouraging only to the extent that a wide variety of plant products, including sunflower oil, rapeseed oil, and soybean oil, would indeed turn a diesel engine and showed an energy content and thermal efficiency almost as high as conventional diesel fuel. But they clogged the engines. They were sticky, and their high viscosity hampered the injection of the oil into the engines. They also charred like oil in a frying pan. After three years of trials with a blend of diesel fuel and sunflower oil, Thomas German of the University of North Dakota reported that he could not recommend the mixture because of the high buildup of carbon deposits in the engine.

A remedy was to change the vegetable oil into combustible soap and glycerol by reacting it with an alcohol, which could itself be made from plant materials. Companies in Britain and in the U.S. explored this process of "esterification." It made the fuel less viscous, chemically more stable, and generally more predictable in its performance, but it added to the cost. At 1985 prices, the modified vegetable fuels would cost diesel-engine operators in the U.S. five times as much as their conventional fuel from the oil companies. But money was not everything, and if farmers could grow and process fuel for their own engines there might be advantages, especially if their farms were to be evaluated as self-reliant, energy-conserving systems.

Diesel himself had cited palm oil. As it happened the tropical oil palms that produced it were being much improved by British and French breeders using tissue-culture techniques. A hectare of oil palms yielded 6 tons of oil a year, in good conditions, and this figure was expected to rise to 7.5 tons. The price of palm oil on the world market was 300 U.S. dollars a ton (1986).

If it could go straight into a diesel tank, with no conversion or distribution costs, that would work out at about 30 cents a liter or $1.50 a gallon. Thinking small, one could visualize a tropical village meeting its needs for liquid fuel from a few hectares of palm oil, at something below the world price.

Any idea of slaking a large part of the world's thirst for gasoline and diesel oil, with fuels produced from plant crops raised questions of a different order. The budgets of land and sunshine were more decisive and less variable than dollar prices for commodities, and making fuel from crops by the technologies of the 1980s seemed extravagant of these natural resources. The world's output of petroleum was running seventy times higher than its production of vegetable oils, and any major inroad into the petroleum market would require huge increases in the areas devoted to energy crops.

A megalomaniac planter wanting to drive the Saudis out of business by replacing petroleum ton for ton with palm oil would need about 3 percent of the Earth's entire land surface. That was equivalent to the territory of Europe (Eastern and Western), or half the area of the United States, including Alaska. (Oil palms would not thrive in Alaska; the comparison was arithmetical.) Putting this another way, to oust the petroleum-extraction industry with palms would require an increase of 30 percent in the total area of land under cultivation in the world.

Although this was not an impossibility, it was unattractive environmentally as well as economically. It seemed foolish to contemplate at a time when other possibilities were multiplying for energy supplies, vehicle fuels, and new feedstocks for the petrochemical industry. Large-scale production of "biofuels" could be a serious error, addressing the wrong problems, and offering a radical biological solution to peculiar difficulties of the industrial cities. It could also blind its enthusiasts to rival developments.

Gray technology had thrown down a challenge to green engineering, in the form of cheap photovoltaic cells made of amorphous silicon. The material was invented in Britain, developed in the U.S., and exploited by the Japanese; it became known worldwide as the power source for "solar-powered" pocket calculators and other gadgets. Even at an early stage of development in the mid-1980s, amorphous-silicon photocells were converting daylight into electricity with an efficiency of 7 percent. As this was already fifteen times better than palm oil, being equivalent in energy capture to more than 100 tons of oil per hectare per year, it set green engineers a formidable target to chase.

Diesel's dream nevertheless persisted among his successors, who were tantalized by the fact that promising automotive fuels grew on trees. It was exactly the kind of challenge to which the new plant-breeding technologies and genetic engineering methods seemed set to respond. One idea that was not farfetched was to breed a gasoline tree.

The spurges (genus *Euphorbia*) resembled cactuses but had a milky sap that was sometimes unusually rich in hydrocarbons chemically akin to petroleum. One species, poinsettia, was valued ornamentally for its scarlet bracts. Other spurges supplied laxatives and, in the case of the Mexican wax plant, candlewax and lubricants. Melvin Calvin, the California biochemist who won the Nobel prize in 1961 for his discoveries about the mechanisms of photosynthesis, commended *Euphorbia lathyris*, which grows well in semiarid conditions, as a fuel source. He also reported, in 1979, that the Amazonian copaiba could be tapped like a rubber tree to give a fuel suitable for diesel engines without any processing.

Biotechnologists remained skeptical, because cultivators would still have to grow a great deal of plant to get a little fuel. If the one-for-one replacement of petroleum fuels by biologically created hydrocarbons was really to be an aim, microorganisms were more promising than palms or spurges. A single-celled alga called *Botryococcus braunii*, that grew naturally in fresh water or brackish water, turned out to consist (water excepted) of up to 75 percent hydrocarbons. Researchers at the École Nationale Supérieure de Chimie in Paris who cultured the alga estimated that it should be possible to produce 60 tons of hydrocarbons per hectare per year, from natural or man-made ponds.

Yields ten times higher than those of oil palms would represent the jump in productivity needed for biofuels, if they were not to make entirely excessive demands on the world's land.

With that proviso, locally grown fuels would promise energy independence to every country and every village. There was no need to stake everything on *B. braunii* itself. Its living machinery for hydrocarbon manufacture—its genes or its enzymes—were likely to interest genetic engineers and industrial biochemists, with a view to incorporating them in other systems. If yields of 80 tons of hydrocarbon per hectare could be achieved, that would represent an efficiency of conversion of solar energy into petroleumlike chemical energy of 5 percent.

The area required to match the output of the petroleum industry would shrink to less than 500,000 square kilometers, an area somewhat larger than California, and about the size of Spain. Translating that to a human scale: The average inhabitant of the Earth could obtain the equivalent of his 700-kilogram share of the world's production of petroleum from a plot of land or water less than 10×10 meters. That was not necessarily small enough to make it self-evidently a good idea, but it would be far better than what happened in Brazil, in the first big drive toward biofuels.

Lessons from Brazil

The Brazilians elected to run their cars on rum. As the boldest pioneers of green machines, they set out in 1975 to replace gasoline by bioethanol—alcohol produced from sugarcane, and therefore from sunlight. They were very determined about it, and Brazilian production of alcohol multiplied twentyfold in less than ten years. By 1984, 400 industrial plants, half of them linked to sugar refineries, were turning out 9 million tons of alcohol a year, saving hundreds of millions of dollars a year on petroleum imports.

Drivers could no longer buy pure gasoline: the choice was between gasoline mixed with 22 percent alcohol and pure alcohol, which cost 30 percent less. Volkswagen factories in Brazil turned out cars adapted to run on bioethanol. It was impressive proof of how resolute government action, backed by massive subsidies and tax exemptions, could transform major industries: in Brazil's case, gas stations and car engines.

The government of Argentina drew up plans to imitate the Brazilian program. In the Pacific, the Philippines, Papua New Guinea, and other sunny tropical countries became excited about bioethanol, while the Japanese let it be known that they might try to replace up to a third of their petroleum imports by alcohol fuels made from cassava or yams grown on the territories of their Asian neighbors.

European governments were interested too. The French selected the Jerusalem artichoke as the best energy crop and planned to grow it on a large scale in order to make acetone-butanol for eking out the gasoline. Heavily subsidized pilot plants for bioethanol production appeared in Sweden and Germany. Engineers of the Volkswagen company, from their experiences in Brazil, commended ethanol to the German people as the automobile fuel of the future. But making sufficient fuel for their cars might mean planting half of Germany with sugar beet, so their advice was, "Buy it from Brazil."

The Brazilians exported some of their bioethanol to the U.S., and the Jamaicans set about building a plant to supply the American market. The U.S. too, had its "gasohol" scheme for adding 10 percent of bioethanol to gasoline. There were three aims: to make use of surplus American corn by turning it into bioethanol, to replace some imported petroleum, and to do away with lead-laden antiknock additives in gasoline. The Carter administration instituted the program but the Reagan administration did not like it, and it was faltering in the mid-1980s. Fewer than half the plants were operating, and the direct and indirect subsidies amounted to a dollar for every gallon of bioethanol. American doubts about making fuels from food were shared elsewhere, and tumbling oil prices were only part of the reason.

Bioethanol stank, literally and metaphorically. The air of busy streets in Rio and São Paulo reeked of aldehydes, sickly sweet vapors produced by the imperfect combustion of ethanol in the cars. And the scheme to which Brazil, more than any other nation, seemed irreversibly committed looked increasingly like an object lesson in how not to go about using green energy.

The aldehydes might in principle be cut by four-fifths with better engine design or by the use of catalyzers. The political ways of thinking and acting manifest in Brazil's bioethanol program looked harder to cure.

The idea of using sugarcane as a source of fuel had been commended enthusiastically by experts and was not inherently foolish: it worked. If, for example, as Melvin Calvin suggested in 1974, sugar growers in Hawaii chose to set up bioethanol stills to make a little fuel for running their farm machinery, that could be sensible. The scene in Brazil was very different. In a country spending a billion U.S. dollars a year on cereal imports, fields devoted to rice and maize were switched to sugarcane. As the area of land devoted to sugar trebled, food imports increased. People in rural communities found themselves working, not as the smart pioneers of a brave new world of biotechnology, but as poorly paid plantation workers. The natural environment suffered too, as waste "swill" from the bioethanol stills polluted the rivers: 13 liters of it for every liter of bioethanol produced, rivaling in quantity all the human sewage in Brazil.

"Bioethanol is an illusion which we should put behind us." So declared the European Council of Chemical Manufacturers' Federations in an appraisal of the Brazilian experience. Even ignoring huge internal expenditures on the scheme, which some experts put at equal to the entire military budget of Brazil, bioethanol was disastrous in respect of foreign trade. The country lost far more foreign exchange by selling less sugarcane abroad, even at the low prices of the 1980s, than it saved by buying less gasoline.

Scanning the other bioethanol schemes, in the U.S. and their own continent, the European chemical manufacturers saw no merit in them either. For those unimpressed by financial or chemical arguments they reasoned in terms of energy. Taking account of the fertilizer and fuel used in producing the crop, and the energy used in the distilleries and for drying the swill to make cattle fodder, the energy inputs needed to produce each liter of alcohol were more than the alcohol's energy content. New technologies might improve the situation a little but the outlook for bioethanol was bleak.

In Brazil itself there were plenty of ideas about how to improve the technology. One was to use other plant materials besides sugarcane in bioethanol production. Another was to pay more heed to the bagasse, the cellulose residues left when the sugary juices had been squeezed out of the sugarcane. Exploding it with steam, like popcorn, could make it much more useful either as cattle feed or as cellulosic material suitable for attacking with enzymes to make more alcohol. Enzymes of the right kind, cellulases, were being genetically engineered by university scientists in São Paolo. Such approaches represented systems thinking about green machines of a kind that was lacking at the bioethanol program's conception.

Apart from making alcohol, sugarcane had many other, possibly more appropriate uses. On behalf of India's huge sugar industry, P. J. Manohar Rao liked to enumerate them. The first call on the bagasse was as a fuel for the sugar factories' own use, although surpluses could go into fuel briquettes for marketing to the public and other industries. As an alternative to burning it, several sugar mills in India were successfully making paper from bagasse, and were encouraging plant breeders to evolve varieties of sugarcane that were more fibrous rather than less. Cubans and others turned bagasse into particle boards to replace wood in furniture making and, experimentally, into high-grade "dissolving pulp" suitable for turning into rayon. The rind of the sugarcane contained a useful wax, but factories in various countries set up to separate and market it failed to compete with other sources of plant wax.

Cattle could eat the green leaves of the sugarcane, and machines developed in North America for stripping the edible pith out of the bagasse were becoming popular. The molasses by-product from sugar factories could also contribute to cattle feed, either directly or for growing yeast for inclusion in the feed. Molasses served as a raw material for making a wide range of organic chemicals, and Quaker Oats of Chicago demonstrated that a variety of agricultural wastes could be turned into furfural, an industrial organic chemical used in manufacturing nylon 66. The Indian sugar industry was starting to make furfural from bagasse.

For people interested in achieving a sustainable world economy based on renewable resources, the Brazilian bioethanol program had seemed like a giant stride in the right direction. It gained plenty of kudos among some environmentalists and their political friends. But, even leaving aside the economic and practical details criticized by the European chemical manufacturers, the scheme was flawed in more strategic ways.

The preoccupations of the well-to-do about private transport and foreign debts were allowed to override the countryman's concern for the proper use of land and the daylight falling on it. There was no serious attempt to work from the ground up in order to integrate bioethanol with local ecosystems and agricultural practices. And the technology of bioethanol production, though well proven, was rudimentary in relation to modern concepts of green machinery, where the aim would be to make the bugs do more of the work, and perhaps to produce not ethanol but gasoline.

To pitch primitive green systems into battle against the formidably sophisticated gray armies of the automobile and petroleum industries did no good at all for the cause of creating a solar civilization. Politicians and bureaucrats in Rio, who could not be trusted even to get the numbers right, foisted the biotechnological program on the fragile Brazilian countryside and its hapless people. That was the most frightening thing: It was a grandiose exercise of biotechnological power by the government of a nation-state.

The Virgin Grasses

The magic seeds of folklore that allowed Jack to climb his Beanstalk foreshadowed in a sense the high-yielding varieties of the green revolution. But the poor peasants in the real-life stories did not always find a happy ending. Even if they were a little better fed, they could easily finish up enslaved by debt. It was a poor magic that slew no giants.

"Give the bloody stuff away!" Bob Geldof said, about the mountains of food created by European farm policies. After his Live Aid concert had raised $70 million for famine relief in Africa, Geldof went to the European Parliament in Strasbourg and promised to "fume and rage and generally behave like a pop star" unless more were done to help the hungry. In the matter of emergency aid to save lives he had a powerful case, yet the unlimited dumping of food surpluses on African countries would depress local prices and harm the local farmers. Karl-Heinz Narjes of the European Commission had an equally powerful case when he said that the aim must be to encourage self-sufficiency in food production.

Ethical objections to using surplus food for the production of fuels or materials, when it might in theory go into the mouths of hungry people, were essentially superstitious—the result of centuries of deprivation. The arguments on this score were sometimes reminiscent of the parental insistence that a child make a clean plate because millions of other children were starving. The smart child replied, "Well, why give it to me?" A gardener could throw away flowers with never a thought, people might happily wear cotton shirts that took valuable land to produce, but if something was edible it ought to be eaten. Expressions of horror at the idea of using food surpluses to make plastics were far off-target when it came to the ways in which green industries might really harm the neediest.

The Third World stood to lose more than it gained from the new biotechnology. The chief threat came from replacements for the common or rare products of plants grown in tropical areas, on which poor countries often relied for earning foreign exchange. The chemical industry's success in making aniline dyes and synthetic rubber spoiled the market for the indigo growers and rubber planters. Biotechnology produced new sweeteners from maize or potatoes, and threatened the traditional sugar exports from tropical countries. The price of a ton of sugar dropped from 633 U.S. dollars in 1980 to 78 dollars in 1984. When genetic engineers transferred into a bacterium the gene for thaumatin, a sweetener traditionally gathered from wild plants in Africa, they gave another twist to the knife. The making of new animal feeds from plant wastes and chemicals in the rich countries cast a shadow over exports of soya (soybeans) from poor countries. The falling demand for cash crops could liberate land for food production, but to think only in those terms reduced the Third World countries to a level of mere subsistence.

Rich countries found it easier to move toward a prosperous self-sufficiency than poor countries. Revenue from the rich mineral deposits in the Third World was also vulnerable to biotechnology because bacteria could be used to concentrate metals in poorer ores within the industrialized countries themselves. Sulfur-loving bacteria treated metal sulfides as food and in doing so made the metals soluble in water. Some 10 percent of U.S. copper production came from bacteria grazing on the normally discarded low-grade residues or "tailings" at the mines. Nickel, silver, and zinc were obvious candidates for similar extraction methods. Organic and ceramic materials were invading areas of engineering such as car manufacture that formerly relied exclusively on metals.

Even the Third World's great asset of cheap labor, which it turned to good account during the rise of the microchip industry, became uncompetitive with the development of industrial robots. While the Ford company generated bold computer-coordinated strategies for scattering factories for vehicles and components into low-wage countries, General Motors turned the other way, seeking to use 20,000 robots to concentrate its manufacture in flexible factories nearer home. Commenting on these developments, Gerd Junne of the University of Amsterdam predicted a shift of production activity back to the industrialized countries and a downward trend in the prices of raw materials. Junne advised developing countries to respond by pooling their research efforts in biotechnology applied to agriculture, in order to reduce their own dependence on imports.

The giants in the agricultural world were the big chemical companies that had a $50 billion business in selling fertilizers and pesticides. A commercial harbinger of the new biotechnology was a spate of takeovers of seed businesses by companies such as Shell, Imperial Chemical Industries, and Hoechst. Altogether, the world's chemical, oil, and food conglomerates bought more than a hundred seed companies, and their quest was for magic seeds tailored to match their businesses and chemical products. Industrial interest in biotechnological opportunities gave a tremendous boost to research. The ideas of the scientists were not just pipe dreams but something expected to make real money, and the early phase of a new technology was just the time when the capitalist system operated at its creative best.

That private profit and humanitarian goals could go together was demonstrated in the career of Henry Wallace, the plant geneticist who, in the 1920s, marketed one of the first of the hybrid corns that came to dominate world maize production. He made a lot of money, but he also masterminded the New Deal farm policies of the 1930s and later had to stand down as Roosevelt's vice-president because he was too left wing. Both suppliers and customers gained when combinations of hybrid seeds and chemical products produced spectacular results for the Third World farmers who could afford to buy them. Oil palms, date palms, and other important tropical crops benefited from the commercial development of improved varieties. The fact remained that stockholders would be shocked by any suggestion that the industrial companies' motives were philanthropic.

Information was power, and Third World countries needed access to information about discoveries, techniques, and options if they were to cope with the biotechnological revolution. At Sweden's Karolinska Institute, the microbiologist Carl-Goran Hedén used the term "bioinformatics" for the broad area of interaction between the life sciences and information technology. The data of interest ranged from the sequences of coding units in the genes to industrial details about the best bacteria for a particular fermentation. Hedén saw computers as a means of storing and distributing the data, and he and his colleagues staged a teleconference via satellite that enabled a hundred professionals in twenty-five countries to compare notes about bacteria and enzymes involved in breaking down wood into simpler chemicals.

The World Centre of Information Processing in Human Resources in Paris laid stress on familiarizing young people in the Third World with microcomputers so that they would not be left behind in the era of information technology. The center's agricultural expert, Dominique Peccoud, wanted to adapt for Third World use the sophisticated programs that told French dairy farmers how best to feed their cows. He also saw tremendous promise in "expert systems," in which the knowledge of the world's best experts was distilled onto disks so that, for example, African farmers could identify diseases in their crops simply by answering a series of questions.

The channels of communication from the realm of science to Third World farmers were highly imperfect—not least because they were sexist. Male experts spoke to male officials in Third World capitals or to ranking males in the villages, but the crucial work of sowing was often done by the hands of women. In a classic study in Liberia, American anthropologists established why women given new seeds by their husbands preferred to cook them for supper. The women were the experts and they had not been consulted. Quizzes showed that women were far more competent in distinguishing different varieties of rice than their menfolk.

The division of labor between men and women varied widely on the farms of different continents and countries, and even from crop to crop, but the role of women was usually more important than male administrators had realized. In central Nigeria, for example, women had the prime responsibility for rice, maize, yams, and cassava, while men took more care of the millet and sorghum. When the Rockefeller Foundation, which had sponsored the plant breeding of the green revolution, wanted to do something forceful about hunger in sub-Saharan Africa, it put a woman anthropologist in charge of the program and favored African women for its field staff.

In any case, a rosy picture of scientists collaborating to solve the world's problems was very different from the reality of academic life in the industrialized countries. Partnerships between university laboratories and industries, with professors serving as consultants or shareholding partners in biotechnology companies, were an effective way of channeling advanced research into productive industry, but academic candor suffered. Laurie Garrett, a science reporter for National Public Radio in the U.S., told in 1985 how he revisited labs in Berkeley and Stanford where he had been a student and found the atmosphere completely changed. The faculty members had aligned themselves with competing companies, and "the departments had become almost like warring camps." Equipment was ear-marked for the service of particular companies, and graduate students were forbidden to discuss their work with fellow students.

This was no atmosphere for the free dissemination and wise use of biotechnological data. When professors wanted to get rich, who should trust their scientific judgment and advice on matters of technology options, or the safety of genetic engineering? Why expect them to impart trade secrets to professionals in India or Senegal when they would not even tell their colleagues in their own universities?

Alarmed by the capacity of Japanese visitors and trading partners to assimilate technical information from U.S. biotechnology labs and turn it into products competing with U.S. industry, American companies agreed among themselves to license products rather than technologies to foreigners. While those genuinely anxious to help the world's poor were trying to maximize the transfer of technology from one part of the world to another, businessmen were trying to minimize it. And academic scientists in the Third World did not shrink from imitating their opposite numbers in richer countries and trying to win a piece of biotechnological profit for themselves.

The conflict between the profit motive and humanitarian aims was plainest in the matter of seeds. The ideal seed for a genetic businessman produced a plant that was sterile, thereby ensuring that farmers would have to go on buying their seeds afresh from his company every year instead of simply harvesting them. Plant breeders wanting to maximize the benefit of new crops to poor farmers were turning to the opposite extreme in plant reproduction: apomixis.

This term meant "without mingling" and it signified a plant equivalent of virgin birth. An apomictic plant did not even need to be fertilized with pollen in order to produce seeds. Ordinary vegetative cells in apomictic grasses, for example, spontaneously turned into seed embryos. The resulting plants were genetically identical with the mother. Having given up sex they were in an evolutionary straitjacket, but that was an advantage for growing a highly predictable crop and avoiding genetic contamination by wild relatives living near the farmers' fields. Many wild grasses, including the bluegrasses, showed a strong tendency to adopt apomixis as their means of reproduction, and the superfluous pollen from an apomictic plant could communicate the habit to other varieties of grass.

When plant breeders introduced apomixis into millet and wheat, the results were genetically messy; they foresaw many generations of breeding to achieve varieties that retained the merits of the standard crop. By definition, an apomictic crop was more difficult to adjust genetically than a conventional plant, although culturing plant cells outside the plant offered a way of generating spontaneous mutations. The big hope was that molecular biologists would discover the genetic and biochemical mechanisms of apomixis so that it could be introduced into crop plants without causing genetic anarchy. Given these magical virgin seeds, poor peasants could multiply them to their heart's content and share them with their neighbors. That was a way to beat the seed companies.

Rivers of Beer

Paradise on Earth for the oppressed poor was always a dream of leisure and plenty to eat. Medieval ballads in Europe advertised Cockaigne, where geese flew about ready-roasted and dressed in garlic. In A. L. Morton's modern rendering in *The English Utopia*, 1952:

> *There are rivers broad and fine*
> *Of oil, milk, honey and of wine;*
> *Water serveth there no thing*
> *But for sight and for washing.*
> *Many fruits grow in that place*
> *For all delight and sweet solace.*

Pieter Bruegel the Elder, in his sixteenth-century painting of Cockaigne's Netherlandish equivalent, *Luilekkerland,* depicted a lake of milk and mountains of dumpling. A pig ran around ready-roasted, and a boiled egg was looking for someone to eat it. The fences were built of sausages, and the roofs were tiled with tarts.

The traditional vision of a land of plenty survived into the twentieth century in American folk songs:

In the Big Rock Candy Mountains,
All the cops have wooden legs,
And the bulldogs all have rubber teeth,
And the hens lay soft-boiled eggs. . . .

. . . There's a lake of stew, and of whisky, too,
And you can paddle all around in a big canoe,
In the Big Rock Candy Mountains.

In his poem "The Happy Townland," W. B. Yeats wrote of rivers of beer, and his image of equality had queens "dancing in a crowd." The British geneticist J. B. S. Haldane quoted Yeats when he looked forward to a coming age of plenty created by microbiology and chemistry. In his book *Daedalus* (1923), Haldane anticipated a time when sugar and starch would be "about as cheap as sawdust." He thought that many foodstuffs, including proteins, would be built up from sources such as coal and atmospheric nitrogen. Agriculture would become a luxury, and synthetic food would substitute the flower garden and the factory for the dunghill and the slaughterhouse.

In a flight of science fiction, Haldane wrote of the Russian invention of a purple alga *Porphyrococcus fixator.* It fixed nitrogen from the air at an unprecedented rate and created a glut of wheat and grazing animals. Then a strain of the alga escaped into the sea. It turned the oceans purple and made fish the universal food.

When he died in self-imposed exile in India in 1964, Haldane left the unfinished manuscript of another work of science fiction, which was eventually published as *The Man with Two Memories* (1976). It described the planet Ulro where the inhabitants lived in cities covered with transparent domes. These enclosed year-round gardens, and most of the living space was underground. The people had learned to create "synthetic life" out of nonliving substances. Some of their food was produced by squeezing pulps and juices from the leaves of specially bred plants that also supplied fibers. The rest came from fungi grown on waste products of every kind; given fungi tasting like beef, there was no need to keep animals except for their milk.

For Haldane, as for Yeats in his more optimistic moments, Cockaigne was a fulfillable dream. But it would not come true painlessly. Just as American folksingers noted the need to hobble the cops in the Big Rock Candy Mountains, Haldane visualized that "atrocious" armed struggles would be needed to bring a better world into being. He summed up his scientific and political views in *Daedalus:*

> The tendency of applied science is to magnify injustices until they become too intolerable to be borne, and the average man whom all the prophets and poets could not move turns at last and extinguishes the evil at its source.

Twenty years after Haldane's death, applied scientists were working hard to surpass his biotechnological expectations. By doing so, they brought nearer the time when the "average man" would lose his patience.

2 POWERS OF LIGHT

SCIENCE'S ugly duckling turned into a swan in Savannah, Georgia, in October 1985. For connoisseurs of academic fashion the First International Congress of Plant Molecular Biology, staged under the dark skies of a tropical storm, was an extraordinary gathering. Was this the botany we knew and pitied?

The study of plants had ranked low in the pecking order for more than a century, even within biology, which of course deferred to physics. Botany's low esteem was not easy to explain. The existence of genes, the very focus of modern biology, was discovered in the 1860s by Gregor Mendel, the botanist monk, using hybrid garden peas. Yet a century later, when plant researchers in the agricultural institutes worked the Mendelian miracle of oversupplying the hungry world with food, the Nobel prize awarded to Norman Borlaug was not for physiology but for peace. As a matter of scientific prestige, this was a put-down for the botanists. Barbara McLintock made a fundamental discovery in the 1940s, that certain genes in maize rearranged themselves spontaneously in a natural form of genetic engineering, but she had to wait for her Nobel prize until 1983, by which time she was over eighty years old.

Ambitious young biologists shared the prejudices of the Nobel committees. They studied microorganisms, animals, or for the surest route to glory, human beings. Teaching hospitals and medical and pharmaceutical research labs had the pick of the talent in molecular biology, and monopolized the expertise. In the public mind botanical gardens were a fancy kind of park, not scientific powerhouses for generating new opportunities for the human species.

An international meeting of plant molecular biologists in Hungary in 1971 attracted only 40 people, but at later meetings in Western Europe many applicants had to be turned away. When Leon Dure of the University of Georgia, as president of the International Society for Plant Molecular Biology, planned the Savannah congress, the intention was to make it open to all comers. About 1800 scientists, mostly young and bright eyed, turned up from thirty-three countries, including China and Peru. Plants were suddenly the scientific flavor of the decade.

Few of these young men and women were botanists of the old school who might distinguish pear and plum trees at a glance. Some would even have to ask, sotto voce, what the difference was between a stamen and a sepal. They were molecular scientists, more at home in the microworld of the living cell, where they worked as the traffic cops of genes and proteins. But in defiance of former prejudices, all the young biochemists, cell physiologists, and molecular biologists hurrying purposefully around in Savannah's Civic Center had placed their scientific bets on green organisms. Leon Dure eyed them like a bluff farmer at a country fair and commented, "Now we have a critical mass of people."

The party in Savannah advertised the new era of green machines. Big chemical companies and agribusinesses sponsored the congress: CIBA-Geigy, Dow, DuPont, Monsanto, Pfizer, and a score of others. The opening lecturer was Monkombu Sambasivan Swaminathan, the plant breeder who had adapted the green-revolution wheats for India, and by that time was running the International Rice Research Institute in the Philippines. He called for an integration of Mendelian and molecular biology to accelerate progress toward "economically and ecologically sustainable food-production systems." The papers and posters, though cast in language of an esoteric science, dealt with such earthy familiars as spinach, potatoes and Mendel's own garden peas.

Plant molecular biology was the hormone that transformed a set of worthy but often boring pursuits into the most invigorating technology of the late twentieth century. Tiresome questions became sexy: How to cope with the high price of energy and diversify the raw materials for industry? How to save the world's wildlife? Or cure Africa's long hunger? How to keep the overproductive farmers in other parts of the world out of bankruptcy? The new botany promised novel answers.

Other advances in molecular biology were pointing to techniques of great value for medicine, pharmaceuticals, and the chemical industry, and within the field of agriculture, too, the molecular biology of microorganisms and animals promised to be as rich in useful results as plant molecular biology. But plants were the chief traps for the energy of the sun. The relationships of human beings with Nature, and of human beings with one another, hinged on the efficiency with which green systems made use of the powers of light.

The mid-twentieth-century advances in agriculture and simple biotechnology, mentioned in the previous chapter, were wrought by agricultural scientists using techniques dating from a time when molecular biology had no significant impact on food crops and the processing of farm products. They reduced roughly by half the area of land required to feed each human being. In effect they made two ears of corn grow where only one grew before, and therefore deserved better of mankind, in Jonathan Swift's words, "than the whole race of politicians put together."

Even the redoubled human numbers expected by the mid twenty-first century could be fed without enlarging the farmlands, just by bringing the world average productivity closer to that already achieved on the best farms with conventional agricultural science. If that were the only aim, the new biotechnology using molecular biology had plenty to offer in the way of speeding up the breeding of new varieties; reducing the need for chemical fertilizers and pesticides; improving the nutritional qualities of crops; and making them less vulnerable to drought, frost, and disease.

The much grander objective on the horizon was that the new biotechnology should enhance the powers of light tenfold in green machines, and so transform the use of land. With the equivalent of twenty ears of corn growing where two grew before, smaller areas than those already under cultivation would meet a much larger part of human needs for energy and raw materials, as well as supplying abundant food. If people chose to do so, they could give back spare land to the tigers and the wolves. However it was employed, a multiplication of yields by ten would bring a major revolution in human affairs, comparable with the transitions from hunting to farming, from stone to metal, and from muscle power to machinery.

The Secret of Life

High expectations were neither farfetched nor surprising, because the discovery of the secret of life ranked among the top few events in the entire history of science and technology. And unlike discoveries about the creation of matter or the behavior of black holes, the usefulness of this new knowledge on a living planet was never in doubt. The medical provenance of the early discoveries meant that people tended to think first of far-out medical applications. It was only a matter of time before even greater prizes in agriculture became apparent.

Each human being, or snail, or plum tree was known to be a marvelous mosaic of small living cells—10,000 billion of them in the human body. Every cell was under the control of its genes, the chemical instructions inherited from parents and collected in packages called chromosomes. The biological renaissance began in 1944 when Oswald Avery and his colleagues in New York found that genes were made of deoxyribonucleic acid, DNA. Nine years later, in Cambridge, England, James Watson and Francis Crick figured out the arrangement of the long, thin DNA molecules, in the famous twisted ladder of the double helix. The "helix" was almost incidental; the "double" was what mattered.

The discovery was that DNA consisted of two strands joined together like a zipper. Each strand was an extended sequence containing four different kinds of units, the four letters of a genetic code, referred to as "bases." In chemical shorthand, the four bases were A, C, G, and T. Life's secret was that any "A" in one DNA strand always linked up with a "T" in the other strand, while "C" always paired with "G." This meant that genetic messages could reproduce themselves reliably and at will. Unzip the DNA, let every base in each strand take on a new partner of the appropriate kind, and you would finish up with two identical double-stranded DNA molecules. This simple but effective trick, repeated countless times, linked human beings in direct lineal descent with the primitive genetic systems of the first bacterial cells of the planet Earth.

Second only to the genes, other key molecules of life were the proteins that carried out essential workaday functions in living cells. These too consisted of long chains made by joining chemical units together: in their case, twenty different sorts of amino acids. In Cambridge, John Kendrew and Max Perutz discovered the three-dimensional architecture of proteins that carried oxygen in animal bodies. Later structural analyses of many other proteins revealed, for example, the configurations that enabled some of them to operate as enzymes for promoting precise chemical reactions within the cells.

The makeup of each kind of protein was described in detail by the genes. As molecular biologists deciphered the genetic code, they found that a sequence of three DNA letters made a word that specified the incorporation of a particular amino acid into a newly assembled protein: for example "CCT" spelled glycine. The DNA did not play a direct part in the manufacture of proteins; instead, molecular strings of a related kind called RNA (ribonucleic acid) took chemical impressions of the genetic instructions and carried them to factories within the cell. There the instructions brought by the messenger RNA were translated into proteins consisting of the proper sequences of amino acids.

As these principles became clear, other discoveries multiplied. Fundamental investigations probed deeper into the machinery of the cells, which handled their molecular traffic like a postal system, and also into the control mechanisms by which individual genes were switched on or off during the life of the cell. Powerful new methods of analysis speeded the tedious work of reading the chemical sequences of genes and proteins. It turned out that genes were often split into segments of DNA separated by irrelevant material. Spoiled genes causing hereditary defects could be identified and characterized, as could the viruses, as rampaging parcels of genes in protein wrappers.

The subtle molecular mechanisms by which cells fought disease or degenerated into cancers occupied many molecular biologists.

That Nature was a genetic engineer appeared in an assortment of discoveries. All of the techniques for manipulating genes that biotechnologists adopted had been employed by natural organisms for millions of centuries. The disconcerting resistance to antibiotics that many bacteria developed when these drugs came into medical use proved to be a case of natural genetic engineering. Bacteria that happened to possess the right gene, enabling them to tolerate an antibiotic, injected it into other bacteria by a process called conjugation, a microbial version of sex.

Viruses, too, were capable of stealing genes from one organism and dropping them off in another. Or a cell could accidentally pick up one of the loose strands of DNA that lay around after other cells died. Such natural events were rare, but Nature had plenty of time to accomplish them. Molecular biologists began to think that evolution should be reinterpreted to include, along with the well-known changes within each lineage of plants or animals, expectable though little known changes due to genes vaulting between the lineages.

Another of Nature's rare but portentous tricks was to fuse two different cells together to make a hybrid cell containing genes from both. Processes of this kind occurred in cancers, for example, and certain influenzalike viruses had a knack for causing cells to fuse together. In 1965, Henry Harris and J. F. Watkins of Oxford announced that they had set Sendai viruses to work on a mixture of cancer cells, human and mouse, cultivated in bottles. They used cancer cells because unlike ordinary cells these were more or less immortal and could be cultured for much longer periods.

These experiments produced hybrid cells "of mice and men" and aroused a public furor about scientists playing God. Research of this kind nevertheless accelerated progress in genetics and cell biology. A sensational payoff from cell fusion came ten years later, with the production of "monoclonal antibodies." Antibodies were molecules tailored by Nature to combine with specific alien molecules (antigens) and so neutralize them. Resistance to viruses, for example, was a matter of deploying anti-bodies. In the natural processes of immunity in humans and other animals, special B-cells manufactured the antibodies. In 1975, César Milstein and Georges Köhler, working in Cambridge, managed to fuse B-cells with cancer cells in a culture. This conferred immortality on the B-cells, and the combined "hybridomas" went on indefinitely making more and more molecules of particular antibodies.

Monoclonal antibodies had obvious and speedy applications for medical and pharmaceutical purposes. In agricultural research, they promised new vaccines against animal diseases and helped plant scientists to identify viruses and bacteria causing diseases in crops. As a laboratory tool, a mass-produced antibody could pick out a rare but valued material from a messy background of other molecules. "Mass-produced" was a relative term: ten years after Köhler and Milstein's discovery, the worldwide output of monoclonal antibodies was about ten kilograms.

Some twenty years after DNA had first yielded its structural secrets, it became fully amenable to cutting and splicing by genetic engineers. It was a matter of using Nature's own scissors (restriction enzymes) to snip out a particular segment of DNA from the genes of one organism. This could then be recombined with the DNA from another organism. In 1973, groups led by Stanley Cohen in Stanford and Herbert Boyer in San Francisco transferred genes from one species of bacterium to another, resulting in the first functional hybrids produced by "recombinant-DNA" technology. Quite apart from the possibilities it opened up for creating novel organisms, the technique became routine in the molecular biology labs as a handy way of "cloning" individual molecules of special interest by introducing the appropriate gene into a bacterium and letting it reproduce itself millions of times.

The safety of recombinant-DNA technology was first debated among the scientists themselves. Paul Berg of Stanford had been leading the development of the new technology until his proposal to transfer genes from a cancer-causing virus into a common bacterium raised eyebrows and hackles among some of his colleagues. On Berg's initiative, molecular biologists declared a moratorium on potentially dangerous gene-splicing experiments until they had figured out how to regulate them and, where necessary, to contain them within physical and biological defenses.

The sense of responsibility shown by the molecular biologists brought them under attack from all sides. Some of their own colleagues, in a hurry to fight human diseases or push back the frontiers of knowledge, thought it a lot of fuss about nothing and a needless brake on their research. More stridently, and with more influence with governments, companies eager to exploit the new biotechnology complained that regulations would hit their profits. In the public arena, antitechnology activists lumped recombinant DNA with the nuclear power industry as a nasty new danger that ought to be stamped out. Religious leaders and others, including many biologists, were perturbed about long-term temptations to modify human beings by genetic engineering.

By the mid-1980s, the controversy about genetic engineering had shifted to a new issue. The restraint and regulations of the molecular biologists had on the whole reassured the public about experiments and manufacturing processes conducted indoors. Biological and physical barriers prevented the escape of modified organisms into the world outside. Applications in agriculture implied the deliberate release of modified organisms into the environment, and this raised awkward questions about the very idea of green machines created with the help of genetic engineering. But for any cool consideration of the risks, it was necessary first to know what kinds of modified organisms—plants, animals, bacteria—the agricultural biotechnologists had in mind.

Genetic engineers began introducing alien genes into crop plants in the early 1980s. Their purposes were experimental, aimed at proving a technique, rather than engineering new crops at the first attempt. Nevertheless, a burst of successes in several laboratories in Europe and North America, announced in 1983, alerted the scientific world to the big changes pending in botany. Every gene transferred in this early batch of experiments penetrated the genetic defenses of the target plants with the help of a sneaky intruder provided by Nature itself.

Galling Ingenuity

Gardeners looking closely at shrubs, vegetables, or flowers growing in wet soil often found the rounded growths of crown gall at the bottom of some of the stems. The unsightly lumps were the work of the "little stick in the fields that makes swellings"—or *Agrobacterium tumefaciens* in the microbiologists' Latin. They occurred when a wound allowed the bacterium, which inhabited the soil, to enter a plant and multiply inside it. The galls were soft in herbs and hard in woody-stemmed plants. Crown gall was widespread, both geographically and in the huge range of broad-leafed flowering plants that it could attack. It was not very harmful, and botanists regarded crown gall as a commonplace, undramatic disease, until it proved to be the work of one of the most ingenious microbes on Earth.

The crown-gall bacterium prospered by genetic engineering long before human beings thought of such a thing. Its molecular detectors sniffed out rare chemicals released by a wounded plant. It would then insert a segment of its own genetic material, DNA, into the plant's hereditary apparatus, in a chromosome within a cell. Then, for the benefit of the crown-gall bacterium, the plant cell went crazy. Imagine space invaders hijacking the Earth's industries and forcing them to produce peculiar chemical foodstuffs needed by the interlopers. Something very like that happened at a microscopic level in plant cells infected with crown gall. The genetically modified cells grew and proliferated rapidly, and manufactured a special material that the bacterium used as its sole source of energy, carbon, and nitrogen.

One strain of crown-gall bacteria commanded, for example, the production of a molecule called nopaline. The DNA inserted into the victim-plant's chromosome included the codes describing an enzyme called nopaline synthase. The plant cell thereupon started making the enzyme, which in turn converted some of the cell's own supplies of energy and materials into nopaline. As this became available, the bacterium feasted on it, using the products of other genes to metabolize the nopaline. Having diverted a small part of the plant's energy to its own purposes, the bacterium multiplied.

The lifestyle of crown-gall bacteria astonished and mystified the molecular biologists. By what evolutionary fluke these humble microbes acquired the genetic know-how for manipulating the genes of far more complicated living organisms, no one could tell. But details of the trick itself became plainer. Each crown-gall bacterium contained a large ring of DNA called the tumor-inducing plasmid, which included the segment of DNA transferred to the plant cell. The segment fooled the plant cell into accepting it as part of its own genetic material. The ends of the transferred segment had sequences of bases in the genetic code very similar to sequences occurring in the plant's own genes. Furthermore, the inserted genes were written in the code used by plants and animals, which differed from the bacterial code in respect of punctuation. That is to say, the DNA included signals in the form of certain base sequences that told the machinery of the plant cell where to start reading the gene ("transcription promoter") and where to stop ("termination signal").

The crown-gall bacterium offered genetic engineers an unbeatable way of introducing selected DNA into any of the very wide range of plants that could be infected by it. If human manipulation introduced a selected gene into the transferable segment of tumor-inducing plasmid, the crown-gall bacterium would then insert the gene into the plant.

Even then, the operation was tricky. It was often a matter of first transferring the chosen gene into a segment of crown-gall DNA in another bacterium (*Escherichia coli*), and then inserting that DNA into the crown-gall bacterium, where it joined up with the tumor-inducing plasmid. The climax of the operation was to set the modified crown-gall bacteria to attack, not a whole plant, but a culture of plant cells.

At a meeting in Miami Beach in January 1983, Josef ("Jeff") Schell from the Max Planck Institute for Plant Breeding Research at Cologne and Marc Van Montagu from the University of Ghent announced that they had successfully transferred into plant cells certain genes that made them resistant to antibiotics—three different antibiotics in fact, with three different genes. The Monsanto company and Washington University reported a similar result with a gene coding for resistance to one of these antibiotics. Nobody suggested that resistance to antibiotics was a valuable property for a plant, but it made it easy to demonstrate that novel genes could indeed be introduced into plant cells and function there. Later that same year, the Agrigenetics Advanced Research Laboratory in Madison, Wisconsin, announced the first successful transfer of a gene from one plant to another. Still using the crown-gall bacterium, the experimenters took out of bean cells the gene for making a protein called phaseolin and inserted it into sunflower cells, which duly began manufacturing phaseolin.

The task remained to regenerate from the infected and modified plant cells whole plants capable of reproducing themselves. The experimenters had first to disarm the crown-gall bacterium, to stop it from creating tumors. This they did by deleting from the infective plasmid a set of five genes that made the plant cells tumorous. The creation of cancer-free crown gall was a signal achievement of Schell, Van Montagu, and their colleagues. Monsanto researchers in St. Louis discovered how to speed up the regeneration of modified plants by inoculating, not separated plant cells, but small fragments of leaf. Scientists also made progress in defining the genetic signals—stretches of DNA—that had to accompany an alien gene if it was to function properly when inserted into a plant. By 1985, potentially useful genes were being transferred into whole plants. The Agrigenetics scientists, for example, put a gene for a seed protein of French beans into tobacco, where the gene functioned correctly and made the protein in the appropriate place—the tobacco seeds.

Monsanto researchers made petunias that were resistant to Monsanto's own herbicide, Roundup. The active agent in Roundup, glyphosate, kills plants by interfering with an enzyme involved in making certain essential amino acids. To the gene responsible for this vulnerable enzyme, Monsanto's genetic engineers appended a segment of DNA from a virus that had the effect of causing the gene to work overtime, producing about thirty times as much of the enzyme as normal. As a result, the genetically engineered petunias survived a spraying with the herbicide while ordinary petunias died. Scientists of Calgene, in Davis, California, achieved a similar result with tobacco plants, by another method. They transferred a gene from a salmonella bacterium that conferred resistance to glyphosate. And in these experiments a different bacterium carried the new gene into the plants—not the crown-gall bacterium but a relative, *Agrobacterium rhizogenes*, that caused hairy-root disease.

The virtuosity of the crown-gall and hairy-root bacteria as natural genetic engineers had one great limitation. They normally attacked only the "dicots," a very large class of flowering plants including such experimenters' favorites as sunflowers, petunias, tobacco, tomatoes, and potatoes. Excluded from the normal range of hosts for crown-gall were the "monocots," a smaller but very important class that included the cereal crops. The archetypes of the two classes were the magnolia and the lily; there were many differences between them but the terms used (shorthand for dicotyledones and monocotyledones) referred to differences in the seeds. Transfers of genes from maize to sunflower and from wheat to tobacco and petunias showed that the genes seemed to be compatible in the two classes. But although Belgian scientists succeeded in transforming one of the monocots, asparagus, with the crown-gall bacterium, different methods were needed for smuggling genes into cereals and other important monocots.

Viruses that caused diseases in plants were candidates to serve as carriers of genes. The wheat-dwarf virus and the maize-dwarf virus, for example, were known to consist of two circles of DNA encapsulated in a pair of protein jackets. Researchers at the John Innes Institute at Norwich, England, found that there was room within the capsules for the addition of alien genes. The plant viruses could certainly infect plants with useful genes, and the possibility existed that these genes would become incorporated into the plant's own genetic material, and so be passed on to later generations.

Mobile genes of the kind that Barbara McLintock discovered in maize in the 1940s also offered themselves for exploitation by genetic engineers. Known as "transposons" they were like built-in viruses carried among the ordinary genes. Peter Starlinger in Germany investigated them and made them a lively subject of research in the 1970s. Transposons occurred in many different organisms in animals as well as plants and first figured in genetic engineering in fruit flies in the early 1980s; modified transposons insinuated bacterial genes into the insects. Many plant molecular biologists dreamed of accomplishing the same sort of gene transfer, especially into monocot plants, including maize itself.

Quite the simplest way to introduce new genes into plant cells was to put them in the food—in other words, to include the DNA in the culture medium used for growing the plant cells in laboratory dishes. Ordinary intact cells did not admit alien DNA, but there were various ways of breaking down their defenses. Enzymes from fungi could destroy the walls of the cell while leaving the contents with a protective membrane. Chemical treatment or electric pulses encouraged the membrane to open its "mouths," or pores, and swallow the big DNA molecules offered to them. Scientists at the Friedrich Miescher Institute in Basel, the Max Planck Institute in Cologne, and Stanford University succeeded in using techniques like these to transform monocot plants. They introduced genes conferring resistance to antibiotics into cells of ryegrass, wheat, and maize.

The problem remained of how to regenerate whole plants from the naked and genetically amenable cells in culture. This was a more difficult task with monocots than with dicots, but Japanese research groups reported success in 1986. One idea for escaping from the limitations of cell cultures was to inject the genes into pollen, using a microscopic syringe, and then to fertilize seeds that would grow in the usual way.

Despite plenty of disappointments, the first few years of gene-transfer experiments in plants went very much better than anyone had the right to expect. Plants seemed to be more amenable to genetic engineering than mammals, for example, especially by the test of whether transferred genes functioned properly in their new owners. But the long years of neglect meant that a great deal of elementary information about plant molecular biology remained to be acquired, if manipulation was not to be a hit-or-miss affair.

Many of the most important plants were dauntingly rich genetically. A wheat cell, for example, contained four times as much DNA as a human cell. The plant scientists needed a plant with relatively simple genetics, to enlarge their general knowledge. In 1985, Elliot Meyerowitz of the California Institute of Technology identified the humble wall cress as the ideal plant for study. It reproduced itself almost once a month, and had an unusually small set of genes, with only one-eightieth of the DNA of wheat. Moreover, the wall cress (*Arabidopsis thalania*) was vulnerable to crown gall, and so open to genetic engineering. Meyerowitz selected two wall-cress strains from Germany for detailed investigation, and botanists expected the wall cress to become as famous as the *Drosophila* fruit flies of the animal geneticists.

The plant molecular biologists were as astonished as any on-lookers by the pace at which their genetic engineering was advancing. Intensive work by a growing army of researchers had established several very promising techniques, even though no new variety of any crop had been introduced to the growers as a result of genetic engineering by the mid-1980s. In view of the range of crops, and features of crops, which the genetic engineers might try to tackle, they were like would-be navigators building small boats of uncertain but increasing seaworthiness, on the shore of an immense ocean. Their laboratory techniques depended heavily on the methods of culturing cells and small fragments of plants in glass bottles. This was a theme in its own right in the new biotechnology of plants.

Cultural Revolutions

The natural habitat of the oil palm, the most efficient producer of vegetable oil, was on the river banks of West Africa. Shortly before World War I, oil-palm plantations sprang up on the island of Sumatra, in Southeast Asia; the seeds came from imported palms whose fronds ornamented the roads of tobacco plantations. In due course Malaysia became the chief exporter of palm oil. By the 1970s the very best oil palms were growing in greenhouses under the gray skies of England, the products of cloning programs carried out with plant tissue cultured in glass bottles.

The idea behind cloning was that each cell of a living organism carried a full set of hereditary information. Therefore biological manipulation could in principle regenerate and multiply fully grown organisms, all genetically identical, from small numbers of cells taken from an individual: Notice the name "micropropagation." The traditional method of growing plants from cut branches rather than from seeds was a primitive form of cloning; it did not work for the oil palm. But cloning from cultures of plant tissue or cells in glass bottles could in any case produce a thousand times as many plants from a single original.

Cloned plants grew true to type, unlike those raised from seeds generated in the random mixing of genes during sexual fertilization by pollen. Moreover, the young plants that resulted were free of diseases carried by viruses, which were often passed on to the next generation of plants by the normal methods of propagation. In some crops, yields shot up dramatically with micropropagation, just by the shedding of the burden of viruses; in African cassava, for example, the gain in yield was 600 percent. Plantations of truly identical plants were, on the other hand, especially vulnerable to attack by new diseases: kill one, kill all. That hazard apart, the grower was assured of neat rows of plants all guaranteed to be as high-yielding as the plant selected as the source of the cloned cells.

Cultures of cells and tissues from plants or animals were similar to the cultures used by microbiologists to grow their favorite bacteria. That is to say, the material was kept alive by immersing it in a nourishing broth. Plant cells had been cultured since the 1890s, but practical applications were slow to follow. The plants cloned commercially by tissue culture, from the 1960s onward, included garden flowers and fruit trees. In these cases, the manipulators took tissue from the shoot tip, or meristem, and used growth hormones to encourage it to branch and multiply.

For the oil palm, Laurie Jones at Unilever's Colworth Laboratory in England found that the best sources of cells were the actively growing roots. In the cloning program that began in 1968, much delicate recipe-testing went into finding a growth medium in which the oil palm cells would thrive. In the end, it had more than thirty ingredients. Growth hormones added to the broth stimulated the root cells to multiply to make a disorderly mass called callus. This could then be split up into many separate cultures. The cells lost their rootlike characteristics and organized themselves into embryos, which in turn developed into plantlets with leaves and roots, ready for planting.

By 1977 the first palms cloned in the laboratory in England were growing in Johore in Malaysia. They turned out to be good yielders, but this was only a first demonstration of the technique. French researchers had a parallel program of oil-palm cloning, at the Boudy laboratory of the Office de la Recherche Scientifique et Technique Outre-Mer, and they achieved their first plantations of cloned plants in the Ivory Coast, West Africa, in 1983. The La Mé research station, chosen for these trials, already had a magnificent collection of oil-palm varieties. The British and French programs promised growers in the tropics a supply of millions of oil-palm plantlets capable of producing at least 25 percent more oil per hectare, just by cloning the best plants already available. The long-term aim was to mass-produce short-stemmed, small-fronded palms, yielding abundant oil of high quality—the product of plant breeding programs. Cloning was an important gift to the plant breeders themselves. It speeded their work and enabled them to test genetically identical plants in many different environments. With accelerated plant breeding the eventual yields could be far higher.

The power of tissue-culture techniques was also apparent in reforestation programs in the U.S., where cells in one liter of a growth medium were estimated to produce enough Douglas firs to cover 5 square kilometers of land. The original products of micropropagation techniques were seedlings that had to be planted individually. Although that could be automated, seeds were easier to handle. Researchers in several countries began thinking of artificial seeds made from cultures of plant cells; the cultured embryos would be coated with a soluble jelly containing nutrients and growth hormones. French scientists at Orsay, for example, made artificial seeds of lucerne (alfalfa) from cultured embryos; when sown, they all grew into plants, just like real seeds. But they did not keep like seeds, and ways had to be found of putting the embryos to sleep for indefinite periods, and reawakening them in the soil.

Without using the fancy gene-injecting methods of the molecular biologists, plant biologists were able to produce novel plants by cell culture. One of the first of these was the pomato, produced in 1978 by an American scientist who fused the naked cells of a potato and a tomato. As a crop plant the outcome was unrewarding—the fruits were very small—but it opened a way of transferring genes that conferred resistance to disease from one plant into the other. Cell culture also enabled breeders to reduce the number and variety of genes in plant cells, for example by culturing pollen grains, which contained only half of their plant's complement of genes. And one of the big weaknesses of plant cells in culture, a tendency to mutate, could be turned to advantage as a source of rare but useful genetic novelties.

The Japanese were the first to recruit plant cells in culture to be industrial workers. If a valuable chemical manufactured by a living plant was what you wanted, why bother growing the whole plant? Culture its cells in a large vat, and they would make the chemical for you. It was a matter of scaling up the laboratory techniques, much as the microbiologists had done in order to manufacture penicillin and other antibiotics. By 1983, Mitsui Petrochemical Industries was marketing the first natural plant chemical produced by industrial tissue culture: shikonin, a red dye also used as an astringent. A German company was planning to culture the famous drug producer digitalis.

The opportunities that these developments opened up staggered imaginative scientists. Had not the old seafarers circumnavigated the world and fought vicious wars in order to snatch the rare flavors of spice plants? Even in the late twentieth century, more than a quarter of medical drugs still came from plants, including painkillers such as opium and cocaine that also supplied huge illicit markets. Other drugs were still being discovered. A new one that controlled leukemia, for example, was found in a periwinkle from Madagascar. And plants were prized for their natural pesticides, their perfumes, their caffeine—if materials like these could be made by culturing the cells of the plants, it would make the users independent of distant ecosystems and long-haul trade routes.

Skeptics pointed out the high cost of plant tissue culture. Unlike bacteria and fungi that owed their powers of spoilage and disease to a robust ability to live on minimal nutrients, plant cells were fussy about their food. They liked coconut milk, for example, which contained growth-promoting agents. Formulating the right culture medium for plant cells of each species, with balanced sources of carbon, nitrogen, minerals, and hormones, was a matter of trial and error.

With the primitive culture technologies of the mid-1980s, plant products seemed to be worth making only if you could sell them at more than $500 per kilo. But researchers who were busy taking the witchcraft out of plant-cell broths expected that the industrial technique would become much simpler and cheaper. Moreover, genetic engineering could make the cultured cells much more productive of the desired chemicals.

With such developments in prospect, the growers of exotic drugs and perfumes would not be the only ones to worry about losing their trade. In Pasadena, California, Brent Tisserat of the Agricultural Research Service was aiming to make orange juice by culturing the vesicles of oranges. And the most vivid premonition of a new era in plant products came with a discovery in Lubbock, Texas.

A graduate student at Texas Tech University was testing cultured cells of cotton plants for resistance to drought and salt, when she noticed that some of them were sprouting cotton fibers. These were growing from two sides of each cell; in the cotton plant the fibers were free to grow only from one side. For Norma Trolinder and her research leaders, J. R. Goodin and Jerry Berlin, the test-tube cotton was unexpected. The Texas Tech team had been the first to produce whole cotton plants reliably from cells, and they were exploiting the technique as an aid to plant breeding, when the cotton plants turned out to be obsolescent.

In announcing the discovery, in October 1985, the team members were themselves at pains to calm any fears among cotton farmers in Texas and elsewhere. They stressed the discovery put them in a good position to find out the genetic and molecular mechanisms that switched on the growth of cotton, and to characterize the enzymes involved in building cotton. The aim, they said, was to improve the quality of cotton produced by the plants. The administrator of the Agricultural Research Service declared that laboratory-grown cotton could not, in his belief, possibly replace ordinary cotton in the near future. Goodin of Texas Tech chimed in: "Farmers will still be plowing, planting, and harvesting their fields for a long time to come."

Whether or not these protestations satisfied the farmers, anyone attuned to the new biotechnology read the signals in the opposite sense. It would be only a matter of time before cotton came from cell cultures in factories. Texas Tech had taken care of its patent rights, and the writing on the farmhouse walls of Egypt, India, the Soviet Union, Mexico, and the United States said: Be ready to get out of cotton.

Goals for Plant Breeders

Tissue culture and genetic engineering combined with other new technologies to accelerate programs for breeding better crop plants. One chemical company, Monsanto, ran 123 growth chambers in which climatic conditions anywhere in the world could be simulated. The Plant Breeding Institute at Cambridge, England, used automated systems for sowing and planting in its fields, and computer analyses made subtle comparisons between the performance of different plants. Molecular techniques of analysis helped in classifying plants and detecting special constituents, including desirable genes and unwanted viruses. By such means the ancient art of the plant breeder was rejuvenated as an exact science.

Conventional plant breeding relied on hybridizing varieties of plants, usually by sexual fertilization. It typically required about twelve generations of backcrossing with parent plants before a new variety was ready for release to the farmers. Because other new varieties were following along behind, in the plant-breeding programs, the useful life of a crop was often shorter than the time taken to develop it. Molecular techniques accelerated the process, and tissue culture provided a more rapid way of selecting varieties with particular properties. The expectation among professionals was that conventional methods would still be needed to nurse and test a new variety to the point where it could be supplied with confidence to the farmers.

What were the plant breeders dreaming of in the mid-1980s? Resistance of plants to agricultural chemicals, already demonstrated experimentally by genetic engineering in the case of the herbicide glyphosate, opened up new possibilities in "minimum till" agriculture. Farmers might obliterate everything except the desired resistant crops from their fields by drenching them with artificial herbicides. For critics this was the wrong direction to go, if the aim was to reduce the farmer's dependence on expensive and harmful chemicals. Monsanto and other chemical companies that backed the experiments saw it differently, of course.

The Food and Agriculture Organization of the United Nations hoped that the grains of cereals that grew in the tropics—sorghum, millet, maize—might be endowed with the glutinous qualities of wheat flour, for the sake of people who had lost their taste for sorghum porridge. Meatlike cereals were another goal. Cereals provided 70 percent of all the human intake of protein, but the quality of the protein was inferior to that of animals, and the relative proportions of the various amino acids were less appropriate to human needs. Theoretically, molecular biologists might reengineer the proteins to improve the amino-acid balances and to make cereals much more nutritious. Another, perhaps nearer, objective was to increase the protein content of potatoes, one of the crops susceptible to genetic engineering by the crown-gall bacterium. In any case, scientists concerned with rice breeding in Asia thought too much emphasis should not be placed on protein; calories were at least as important, and vitamins more so.

Many crop plants succumbed to unfavorable weather resulting in very wet or very dry soil, or extremes of heat or cold, while large areas of the Earth were hard to cultivate because of too much salt or poisonous metal in the soil. In all these cases, some plants, many of them wild, survived where others wilted or died. In principle, their resistant qualities might be transferred to crop plants by genetic manipulation. Although there was deep ignorance about the genes involved in resistance to environmental stresses, hints of the possibilities came from Peter Albersheim at the University of Georgia. He identified carbohydrate molecules that served as signals and regulators in living plants, and suggested that crops could be taught to grow deeper roots to improve their resistance to drought, while orange trees vulnerable to cold could be told to go to sleep in the winter. But such control might be accomplished more easily by spraying the crops with the appropriate chemical signals than by modifying them genetically.

Plant breeders waged a nonstop war against plant diseases, in which novel varieties offering some resistance were soon outwitted by evolutionary changes in the insects, bacteria, fungi, and viruses that caused the diseases. The new biotechnology offered more radical strategies for achieving longer-lasting resistance by encouraging the plants to counterattack. Certain plants, including the neem tree and the pyrethrum flower *Chrysanthemum cinerariaefolium*, produced natural insecticides, and so did some bacteria. The bacterium *Bacillus thuringiensis* produced agents that killed the larvae of moths, and genetic engineers conferred the relevant bacterial genes on tobacco plants. Genes coding for antimicrobial and antiviral agents might also be introduced into crop plants.

More subtle goals for plant breeders included altering the growing seasons of crops. This might achieve better yields or more harvests per year, or make the crops suitable for new environments. In response to the drive for farm automation in industrialized countries, other modifications in plants made them easier to harvest by machines. For those concerned for the needy of the world, the main task was to produce, not high-yielding crops that needed pampering in the high-tech style of European and North American agriculture, but tough crops that would give fairly good returns in poor soil and harsh environments, with a minimum of chemical inputs. The greatest ambition of some genetic engineers was to make crops independent of artificial fertilizers for the nitrogen essential to their growth.

Self-nourishing Crops and Farms

Because the increases in crop production during the agricultural revolution of 1960–85 depended on ever heavier applications of artificial nitrogenous fertilizers to the soil, these became a source of pollution in rivers and lakes. The fertilizers were also costly to produce in terms both of money and energy, although they remained cheap in relation to the added value of the crops. The world's poorest farmers could not afford them, and farmers in industrialized countries were using a hundred or even a thousand times more fertilizer per hectare than their counterparts in the least fortunate parts of Africa. The irony was that nitrogen, the most abundant gas in the Earth's atmosphere, ought to have been readily available to farmers everywhere.

Genetic engineers wanted to endow crop plants with a capacity to fix their own nitrogen directly from the air so that they would become self-nourishing in this respect. The scientists' chief mentors were the humble bacteria that captured nitrogen far more slickly and with less expenditure of energy than the chemical engineers' fertilizer factories. Living in the soil and the roots of certain plants, including beans and clover, these bacteria were able to absorb the nitrogen gas from the air and turn it into a form that plants could assimilate.

The bacteria's level of activity set a limit to the natural productivity of the land. From a geochemical point of view, what was happening during the latter part of the twentieth century was a wholesale conversion of energy—typically from oil—into nitrogenous fertilizers needed to feed the soaring numbers of human beings on the planet. At 90 million tons a year (1985), or 20 kilograms for every person on Earth, these added perhaps 50 percent to the nitrogen fixed by natural means on the entire planet.

Even without genetic engineering, by selecting and distributing the most effective strains, agricultural researchers could help farmers to make better use of existing nitrogen-fixing bacteria. Farmers in parts of Southeast Asia traditionally inoculated their rice paddies with cyanobacteria (blue-green algae), which fertilized the crop, and tests in the Philippines confirmed that artificial fertilizers were unnecessary if the bacteria performed as they should. For this reason, the huge differences in fertilizer consumption in various parts of the world had to be interpreted with caution.

In modern guise, selected strains of cyanobacteria were marketed as fertilizing agents in the U.S. and elsewhere. Yields of clover on the Welsh hillsides and of soya (soybeans) in the fields of Italian farmers benefited from inoculation with improved strains of the symbiotic *Rhizobium* bacteria, developed in Britain as more efficient nitrogen-fixers. The Food and Agriculture Organization and the UN Environmental Program promoted similar inoculations for Third World crops, using better bacterial strains. In Senegal, inoculations more than doubled the yields from soybeans. But the genetic engineers had more radical possibilities in mind.

A landmark in early research was the first transfer of genes responsible for nitrogen fixing, from one bacterium to another. This was accomplished in 1972 at the University of Sussex in England, by a group led by John Postgate. It inspired greatly intensified efforts, especially in the U.S. where the biological fixation of nitrogen became a top research priority for the Department of Agriculture. Knowledge of the molecular biology of the nitrogen-fixing system increased rapidly, and it turned out to be very similar in all the bacteria that possessed it. At the same time, the problems of exploiting this knowledge became, if anything, more daunting.

Glittering prizes were thought to await the successful production of nitrogen-fixing rice or wheat. The genetic engineers saw two main routes to this target. The first was to extend into other crop species the symbiosis that allowed nitrogen-fixing bacteria to live in the roots of beans. There was great uncertainty about what genetic changes might be necessary in the plants or the bacteria or both, to bring this about. For example, beans supplied a special product, leghemoglobin, which protected the nitrogen-fixing system of the bacteria from damage by oxygen. A hopeful sign for the future was that some grasses in the tropics had achieved a natural symbiosis with nitrogen-fixing *Azospirillum* bacteria.

Another road to self-nourishing crops led by way of more radical genetic engineering aimed at introducing the nitrogen-fixing genes into the plants themselves. This was a formidable task. At least seventeen different genes were involved in nitrogen fixation in the best-known bacterium, the free-living *Klebsiella pneumoniae,* and these would have to be persuaded to operate in a concerted fashion in a novel setting inside the plant. Other genes evidently played a part in their regulation.

By the mid-1980s, experts thought their best hope was to introduce the nitrogen-fixing genes into bacterialike compartments inside plant cells, called chloroplasts. These were also the plant's traps for solar energy. Chloroplasts had their own system of heredity, which resembled the genetic systems of bacteria much more closely than the main genetic systems of the plants, and this increased the chances that the nitrogen-fixing genes could function there.

Skeptical biotechnologists pointed out that the plants would pay a price for their nitrogen in terms of the energy they would have to supply to the system that fixed it. This would be reflected in lower growth rates. These critics said that nitrogen-fixing plants were not only very difficult to engineer, they were probably undesirable anyway.

The goal in nitrogen fixing had to take account of local circumstances. Isolation or poverty might make lower-yielding but self-sufficient plants attractive, but not if cheap nitrogen fertilizers were available from biological or chemical sources. Applying artificial fertilizers to the leaves of crops instead of the soil was known to increase their effectiveness from 20 to 85 percent. According to Robert Eibner of the Schering company in Duesseldorf, the world's wheat harvests could be increased by 10 percent by leaf fertilization.

Chemists at the U.K. Agricultural and Food Research Council's Unit of Nitrogen Fixation, housed in the University of Sussex, announced in 1985 a new inorganic method of fixing nitrogen from the air. It promised to be suitable for the small-scale manufacture of fertilizer. The traditional process, invented by Fritz Haber in Germany some seventy years earlier, caused nitrogen and hydrogen gas to react together to make ammonia, but it required high temperatures and very high pressures and the use of special catalysts. The technique invented in Sussex worked at ordinary temperatures and pressures.

Ten years previously, the Unit of Nitrogen Fixation had discovered that certain chemical compounds based on tungsten could take up nitrogen gas and then react with an acid to make ammonia. The problem was to recycle these "dinitrogen complexes" in some simple fashion so that the ammonia production could proceed without interruption. Christopher Pickett and Jean Talarmin found they could keep regenerating the material by means of an electric current while making ammonia continuously.

Although a lot of chemistry and engineering remained to be done to turn this into a practical system, Pickett and Talarmin looked forward to small electrical reactors driven by solar cells that might enable farmers anywhere to make their own chemical fertilizer. No parting of the ways between the chemists and the molecular biologists in the matter of nitrogen fixing was implied by this development. On the contrary, the chemical work at Sussex suggested possibilities for altering and simplifying the natural nitrogen-fixing machinery. That might make it easier for genetic engineers to handle, if self-nourishing crops remained the goal.

Engineered Animals

The successes of conventional plant breeding in the period 1960–85 were paralleled by improvements in the performance of farm animals. In Europe, the volume of milk produced by each dairy cow doubled. Artificial insemination was one of the techniques that accelerated the testing and multiplication of more productive animals. R. B. Land of the Animal Breeding Research Organisation in Edinburgh thought milk yields could redouble during the next quarter century.

Great expectations surrounded methods for manipulating embryos of farm animals. These were like the techniques used in producing human "test-tube babies" but without the same ethical constraints. Embryo manipulation made possible the predetermination of the sex of young animals and the production of identical twins by cutting very young embryos in two.

Other experiments aimed at producing chimeras—mixed-up animals—by combining embryos from two different species. By the early 1980s researchers at Giessen, Germany, had produced a goat from a sheep mother, while others in Cambridge, England, were creating full-fledged sheep-goats. One of these, a very woolly animal, looked like a goat in sheep's clothing, and its blood contained proteins belonging to both parent species. In contrast with the earlier cell-fusion techniques, the embryo-mixing method gave rise to two distinct cell lineages (sheep and goat) that remained intact but scattered through the animals. Protesters paraded outside the Cambridge lab's headquarters with signs reading NO MORE SHOATS, but the experimenters claimed a benign objective in their work: the saving of endangered animals by breeding them in mothers of other species.

Ralph Brinster of the University of Pennsylvania and his colleagues produced giant mice in a striking demonstration of genetic engineering in animals. These were the result of injecting into fertilized mouse eggs a clone of engineered DNA, consisting of a growth-hormone gene from a rat coupled to a regulating gene from a mouse. The injection "took" in about a quarter of the cases. In 1985, the same group reported the first transfer of a gene into farm animals by injection of eggs. They used a human gene coding for the growth hormone, again coupled to a mouse regulator gene. Results in sheep were disappointing, but the experimenters were able to get the growth-hormone genes working properly in several pigs. There were no spectacular effects on the growth of the pigs, but genetic engineering in farm animals was a proven possibility.

Imagination then set the only limits to what might be accomplished. More fertile female animals were one objective of the researchers. Certain merino sheep in Australia and New Zealand ovulated at an unusually high rate and produced large litters; the genes responsible might be transferred into cattle, for example. Undramatic but useful improvements in animals could include better resistance to disease, alterations to the physical characteristics of hair or hide, or man-made changes in the nutritional qualities of milk, eggs, and meat.

Cows as chemical factories were another idea. The genes for making particular chemical products—insulin, for example—might be engineered into the animals in such a way that they would find their functional expression in the mammary glands. Then the insulin, or whatever the chosen product was, would come out in the milk.

Jokers suggested that sheep should be equipped with arms and taught how to knit, yet at the dawn of genetic engineering in animals it was easier to understate than overstate the possibilities. Perhaps the physicist Freeman Dyson was nearer the mark than cautious prophets when he proposed Mining Worms that would dig into clay or metal ores and bring wanted materials to the surface, or Scavenger Turtles with superhard teeth that would chop up "human refuse and derelict automobiles."

Much of the early effort in biotechnology applied to animals was directed to fighting diseases, by vaccines and other means, in parallel with the development of molecular biological techniques in human medicine. And just as plants might be controlled by spraying them with chemical messages rather than by genetic engineering, so farm animals were susceptible to chemical management. Routinely, British farmers increased beef yields by 15 percent with hormone implants. In trials in the U.S., milking cows injected with growth hormone every other day produced 30 percent more milk without any increase in their feed. Fear of harm to consumers, especially children, led the European Parliament to vote to ban growth hormones, even though experts pointed out that the amounts eaten were far smaller than the natural production of the equivalent hormones in children.

Were cows necessary? One long-term possibility was to dispense with the whole animal, just as cell culturists were beginning to make plant products without the plants. The proposition that milk-producing glands and meat tissue might be cultivated in vats was not scorned by all biotechnologists. Ungruesome methods of culturing blood might make it fashionable again as a foodstuff—as it was in ancient Greece and still is in Africa and Asia.

By analogy with the production of cotton fibers in cell cultures, the silk glands of the silkworm could be set to work spinning its most prized of natural fibers. By the 1980s, Japanese molecular biologists had largely exposed the silkworm larva's secrets and shown how the natural polymers aligned themselves and solidified under the shearing stress of being squirted slowly through the spinneret in the larva's head. If cultured silkworm glands could be persuaded to perform in artificial media, the ancient quest for mulberry leaves might be ended, and the silkworms left in peace to get on with their proper function of making moths.

Mighty Microbes

A humble fungus outshone all the cultured plants and genetically engineered animals, in some biotechnologists' estimation. What ignited their admiration was the ability of the whiterot fungus, *Phanerochaete chrysosporium*, to chew up wood— not with the clumsy mandibles of a termite but by a chemical attack on the lignin cement that bound the cellulose microfibers of wood together. This was a destructive appetite shared by very few microorganisms—which was just as well, otherwise wood might be worthless as a building material and the world's forests would be in mortal danger. Properly used, the weapon of white rot might be the key to unlock the chemical riches of the biosphere for industrial use.

Of the total mass (water excluded) of living things on land, lignin itself contributed about a quarter, and it bound about three times its own weight of cellulose in tough composites such as wood and straw. In fact, lignocellulose made up 95 percent of the biomass, and was the commonest constituent of plant wastes. To talk of using starch, sugar, and other more tractable plant materials as new feedstocks for the chemical industry, when the abundant lignocellulose might be tapped, was like gathering firewood on top of an oil well. But how to break it down into useful chemical fragments?

The lignin itself was a natural plastic made from chemical units connected in a random fashion. The main units were six-atom rings of carbon atoms (benzene rings) ornamented with oxygen atoms backed by hydrocarbon fragments—the so-called methoxyl groups. Chemically and physically tough, lignin was the more resistant to attack by microbes because its irregular structure gave ordinary enzymes nothing predictable to bite on.

The white powder of denuded cellulose, which gave white rot its name, testified to the ability of fungi to overwhelm the lignin's resistance. *P. chrysosporium* itself flourished on sawdust, while other species decorated fallen trees and logs with multicolored fungal flesh—some of it edible. Within the natural economy, white-rot fungi played a crucial role in putting the carbon from dead wood back into circulation. Some experts suspected that the fungi were kept under control by their own capacity to attack tough organic materials. If they became too potent, they would self-destruct.

John Palmer and his associates at Imperial College, London, investigated the chemical weapon of white rot. They found that the enzyme ligninase in *P. chrysosporium* had the extraordinary power of setting lignin to attack itself. It used hydrogen peroxide to turn one of the main units of lignin into a highly reactive chemical, and chopped it free. This started a chain reaction in which other broken pieces of lignin became chemically activated and widened the circle of damage.

The rare talent of the ligninase enzyme made the chemists keen to mass-produce it for industrial use. In principle it could turn lignin itself into a valuable source of aromatic carbon molecules while liberating the cellulose from wood and straw. Other scientists were busily preparing new ways of exploiting the long carbohydrate molecules of cellulose. One was to turn them into man-made plastics and fibers: celluloid and rayon had for long been produced from cellulose. A newer plastic derived from plant material was polyhydroxybutyrate, developed by Imperial Chemical Industries in Britain. A bacterium, *Alcaligenes euthropus*, manufactured it while feeding on starch and sugars, and one of the plastic's virtues was that it was biodegradable. But this was only a foretaste of new opportunities in polymer biotechnology.

American biochemists used enzymes extracted from another fungus, *Trichoderma reesii*, to break down the molecular chains of cellulose into glucose and other sugars. Yeast could then convert the glucose into ethanol for use either as a fuel or a chemical feedstock. Gulf Oil, one of the companies looking to the possible replacement of petroleum in chemical manufacture, pursued this technique. The lignin remained a nuisance in these processes rather than a source of chemicals in its own right. When Japanese biochemists included it in itemizing the chemicals that might be manufactured from degraded wood, they left no doubt as to the technical possibilities. One could make polymers such as nylon and polyester, or synthetic rubber, or detergents, or dyes and perfumes, or amino acids, or vitamin C, or agricultural chemicals.

Any euphoria about plants as a major source of chemical raw materials was premature. Quite apart from the unfinished technical tasks of making practical systems for converting the wastes, the oil and petrochemical industries set formidable targets to beat in the matter of cost. A report for the EEC's FAST study in 1982 declared flatly: "European agriculture will not become a major supplier of mainstream feedstocks: there is insufficient land area available and the costs would be too high." Oil and natural gas were still seen as the ideal cheap raw materials, and coal was ready to replace them when they became scarce. In this perspective, farm products were expected to supply modest though increasing quantities of "medium-value" organic chemicals by biotechnological routes.

The judgment was sound enough if the aim was to go on running the same chemical industry in the same ways. These had evolved to receive the output of oil refineries and to process them in high-temperature chemical reactions promoted by inorganic catalysts. There was little hope of meeting the industry's traditional needs for raw materials (ethylene, propylene, butadiene, and so on) economically and on a large scale by a biological route. But if one looked not to the inputs to the chemical industry but to its outputs (plastics, fibers, dyes, paints, explosives, and so on) the picture changed. Biotechnologists or solar chemists could offer alternative routes to those desired products, or substitutes for them.

French chemists scanned the natural world for valuable chemicals appearing ready-made in microorganisms. Besides the hydrocarbons from *Botryococcus* already mentioned, these included acrylic acid in *Phaecocystis,* sorbitol in *Dunaliella,* and triglycerides in *Neochloris.* The chemicals used in agriculture itself could be replaced, at least in part, by nitrogen-fixing bacteria and microorganisms producing natural pesticides. Monsanto scientists took an insecticidal gene from *Bacillus thuringiensis* (long used as a biological weapon against caterpillars) and transferred it into a soil bacterium, *Pseudomonas fluorescens.* It would be capable of disinfesting the soil around the roots of crops. Ecological scientists expressed anxiety about the harm it might do to benign insects.

Both as producers and modifiers of materials, microorganisms had a limitless role to play in the new biotechnology. This was only fitting as they were the mainstay of the old biotechnology, from the invention of brewing and bread making onward. By 1980, major industrial products from microorganisms included antibiotics and amino acids such as lysine. Notable newcomers were enzymes from bacteria that broke down starch. These were adopted for the large-scale manufacture of sweeteners from starch, which replaced ordinary sugar in many foods and drinks.

As diminutive industrial chemists, microbes often worked better if they were immobilized, for example by binding them in a plastic foam. They could then deal with materials flowing past them, and continuous processes could replace the traditional batches of the microbiologists. The Japanese led the way with this technique by immobilizing individual enzyme molecules extracted from their living owners, so cutting the cost of amino-acid manufacture by 40 percent. By the 1980s, the pinioning of microbes and enzymes was becoming standard practice in labs and factories.

Microorganisms could be used as food in their own right,

under the name of single-cell protein, to be served up either to human beings or farm animals. In Aztec times in Mexico, people made biscuits out of mats of cyanobacteria called *Spirulina*, which they harvested from alkaline lakes. By the 1970s *Spirulina* was known to be exceptionally rich in protein, and harvesting resumed in Mexico. Italian microbiologists discovered that they could prolong the growing season for *Spirulina* by cultivating it in polyethylene tubes, and they reported production rates of 50 tons per hectare per year—roughly ten times the yields of ordinary crops. Doing without sunshine, Imperial Chemical Industries grew bacteria (*Methylophilus methylotrophus*) on methanol and marketed them as Pruteen.

Few environments were so barren or harmful to life that microorganisms were entirely absent. Bacteria accustomed to living at high temperatures in hot springs were well suited to the production of biogas from animal manure and human sewage in biogas plants running at up to 60°C. Other bacteria thrived among heavy metals that would kill most organisms. They drew sustenance from a range of energy-releasing chemical reactions that seemed strange to animals with more limited tastes. *Thiobacillus* bacteria, for example, could grow by stealing electrons from metal atoms and using them to buy carbon from carbon dioxide. Such microbes were used commercially for winning metals from low-grade copper ores, and experimentally for concentrating uranium from sea water.

Bacteria were always the planet's cleansing agents. Under human management they played a routine part in purifying fresh water contaminated by sewage and industrial wastes. Botho Boehke of Aachen found that purification plants could be made far more effective by excluding large microorganisms that preyed on the bacteria. Bacteria in the sea and the beaches destroyed oil spills, whether from natural leaks or wrecked supertankers. In their cleansing role, bacteria attracted the attention of genetic engineers, with Ananda Chakrabarty of General Electric in the U.S. leading the way.

In the early 1970s, Chakrabarty gathered genetic elements (plasmids) from four different bacteria and combined them in one oil-eating "superbug." This created a stir because in 1980 it became the first genetically engineered microbe to be patented. In 1981, Chakrabarty created another bacterium that broke down the persistent herbicide 2,4,5-T, which was used as an environmental weapon in the Vietnam War and was responsible for serious pollution in the U.S. and Italy. By 1985, Ken Timmis and his colleagues at the University of Geneva had engineered a bacterium to break down another persistent chemical pollutant, methylchlorophenol.

The chemical repertoire of natural microorganisms, already enormous, could be enlarged almost indefinitely by genetic engineering. Bacteria could, for example, replace plants and animals as the source of valuable chemicals. The first commercial process of that kind made rennin in a bacterium. Rennin was an enzyme found naturally in the fourth stomach of a calf, and cheese makers needed it for curdling milk. Genetic engineers of Celltech in England transferred the gene coding for rennin production into the bacterium *Escherichia coli,* which thereupon manufactured rennin abundantly. After treatment with acid (as in the calf's stomach) the engineered rennin had the same effect on milk as the natural enzyme.

"Protein engineering" was the tag under which molecular biologists declared their hopes of going beyond the transfer of existing genes from one organism to another, to the creation of novel genes for making useful enzymes and other proteins. This idea was being pushed hard by a protein-engineering "club" of university and industrial scientists in Britain in the mid-1980s. The chief impediment was ignorance of the natural rules governing the shapes and behavior of protein molecules; on the other hand, devising novel proteins was a good way to learn. Then the way would be clear to improve the efficiency of natural enzymes and to develop completely new enzymes to carry out tasks prescribed by the chemists, for human purposes.

Genetic engineering could also mitigate harmful effects of bacteria. A case in point was *Pseudomonas syringae,* a bacterium that occurred on the leaves of plants. Steve Lindow of the University of California at Berkeley found that it caused frost damage to the leaves because the bacterium carried a protein on its jacket that made an ideal nucleus for the formation of ice crystals. Lindow and Nicholas Panopulos found the gene responsible for this ice-nucleating propensity and deleted it by genetic engineering. Thus they produced a strain of *P. syringae* that did not provoke ice crystals to form; they called it "ice-minus." Lindow's plan was to spray it on fields and orchards in the hope of replacing the harmful bacterium with its man-made "ice-minus" cousin, thus protecting the crops. But he was to be thwarted when an environmentalist came on the scene with a restraining order from a federal court.

The New Debate About Safety

Jeremy Rifkin, author and activist, won court rulings in 1983 and 1984 that prevented Steve Lindow from testing his "ice-minus" bacteria in the open air. For more than two years, as the law took its course, genetic engineering for agricultural purposes remained suspended on the brink of its first field trials. Rifkin's name was reviled in some quarters. Academic scientists resented the doubts cast on their own judgment; agrochemical businessmen investing heavily in genetic engineering complained about the threat to their profits. But the more loudly the new biologists proclaimed their ability to change the world, the greater was the onus on them to convince their fellow inhabitants of the planet that they would not wreck it.

   Genetic engineering made many people deeply uneasy. They had moral scruples about the sanctity of natural life, objected to scientists playing God, worried about the likelihood that humans would become subjects for genetic engineering, and expressed practical anxieties about dangerous man-made organisms breaking loose. There was no doubt about the power that provoked these fears. An advertisement from a Swedish company appearing in scientific journals in 1985 said it all:

> At last! An easy-to-use gene machine at an affordable price. Now any laboratory working with oligonucleotides can perform automated DNA synthesis simply, reliably and affordably—whatever

the volume demand—with the new Pharmacia Gene Assembler™.

A decade earlier, in the great debate about recombinant DNA, the scientists had allayed public fears by sealing in potentially dangerous experiments. Now they were proposing to go to the opposite extreme, by scattering genetically engineered organisms across the landscapes of the world. During the moratorium that Rifkin's legal battle imposed on agricultural biotechnology, many of the sharpest questions came from scientists of repute.

The concern was not confined to the U.S. The release of genetically engineered organisms into the environment was prohibited in a number of countries, including Switzerland where Ken Timmis was developing his antipollution bacteria. The Organization for Economic Cooperation and Development in Paris, which linked the rich industrial nations of North America, Europe, and Japan, labored to try to produce guidelines for safety and regulation in biotechnology. The Reagan administration thought its European partners were taking too negative a view of the new opportunities in biotechnology.

The opinion spectrum extended from those who detested the very idea of genetic engineering, to industrialists who wanted no regulations at all. Molecular biologists and professional ecologists argued the issues at scientific meetings in Philadelphia and Helsinki during 1985. In these discussions it became plain that grounds for great caution existed, but probably not for a total ban on the release of engineered organisms.

Imaginative horror stories helped to focus the mind. Suppose a new nitrogen-fixing bacterium were so successful that it covered the oceans with a deadly scum. Or visualize a genetically engineered wood-eating bug equipped with the potent ligninase enzyme escaping from a factory and destroying all the world's forests. Or consider, as Rifkin himself argued, that Lindow's "ice-minus" bacterium might so spread and multiply as to interfere with the natural processes of ice formation in the atmosphere, altering the world's climate.

Although gung-ho genetic engineers dismissed them as science fiction, such scenarios made salutary points. First, a very small chance of a very great catastrophe ought to be treated as a non-negligible risk. Again, organisms were no respecters of national frontiers, and misguided operations in one country could bring disaster to many others. And in the narratives of the horror stories the perpetrator was often an irresponsible scientist who did not tell his colleagues what he was doing.

Much depended on candor and openness of the kind that Lindow himself displayed, but that in turn relied on the existence of free societies. Even there, commercial secrecy could conceal the uses being made of engineered organisms. Differences in policies between the nations showed that the anarchical organization of the world into nation-states offered scant protection. If a truly mad genetic engineer were bent on a truly dangerous experiment he could find a haven somewhere on the planet.

Wise biologists remembered disasters from pre-DNA days: the European rabbits breaking loose in Australia; the water hyacinth from South America, introduced into Africa as an ornamental plant, spreading to clog the rivers and lakes of that continent; the African killer bees that escaped from a genetics lab in South America and, again, took over a continent. These events were not science fiction, even though they sounded like it. Nevertheless, genetically engineered plants and animals would at least be visible and perhaps killable, if they threatened to get out of hand.

That could not be said for genetically engineered microbes released into the environment. In some forms, microbes could not even be detected by culturing in the laboratory. And their capacity to spread was notorious. A scientific critic of the proposed field trails of the "ice-minus" bacterium, David Pimentel of Cornell University, pointed out that insects picked up the normal *Pseudomonas syringae* bacteria from the plants where it lived. If, as a result of the experiments, harmful insects became less vulnerable to freezing, or beneficial insects such as honeybees were made more vulnerable, the consequences could be grave.

Bacteria were also far more likely than plants or animals to engage in natural genetic engineering on their own account. The transfers of genes that conferred resistance to antibiotics to many species of bacteria were a case in point. Ken Timmis even advertised his hope that, if he introduced gene-spliced bacteria for curing methylchlorophenol pollution, they would pass on their talent to other soil bacteria. Robert Goodman of Calgene was one of many who argued that the only difference between what molecular biologists were doing in the lab and what happened in nature was that bacteria were better at it than the scientists. The fact remained that gene swapping between bacteria meant that the ultimate destinations of engineered genes were unpredictable.

A consensus that emerged between moderate gene-splicers and moderate ecologists was that a total ban on the release of genetically engineered organisms was unreasonable in view of the benefits they might bring; on the other hand, great prudence was needed and ought to be enforced with some measures of regulation similar to those governing the introduction to the marketplace of new foodstuffs and pharmaceuticals. Delays were necessary for thought, for scientific debate, and for appropriate laboratory experiments and field studies. Ecologists were, in the end, reassured about the "ice-minus" bacteria when mutants of *Pseudomonas syringae* turned up in the wild. These also lacked the capacity to nucleate ice crystals and seemed to be doing no harm. In a backhanded fashion, Nature approved the experiments by showing them to be unoriginal.

Rifkin struck again in 1986, in a lawsuit to try to block the sale of a genetically engineered live-virus vaccine against pseudorabies in swine. The U.S. Department of Agriculture had violated the rules in not notifying its own Agricultural Recombinant DNA Research Committee before approving the vaccine. Meanwhile, in Britain, David Bishop of the Institute of Virology in Oxford won official permission to spray a hundred trees in northern Scotland with a modified virus active against larvae of the pine moth. In the first instance, the genetic engineers merely marked the virus with an ineffectual but distinctive genetic tag, so that they could trace how it spread in the environment. This experiment was intended as a prudent preliminary to arming the virus with toxin-producing genes.

The prospect, then, was of never-ending scientific and administrative examination of proposals for releasing new organisms. As case law accumulated, wisdom might deepen. But while many Europeans wanted the onus of proof to rest heavily on the inventors of new organisms, the U.S. administration preferred a framework in which it was up to the regulatory agencies to intervene if they saw a risk. At the Savannah congress on plant molecular biology, government officials were at pains to reassure the scientists that they wanted to impede them as little as possible. National differences in policy and secrecy in commercial operations seemed likely to frustrate the good intentions of the scientists. For better or worse, yet another scientific genie was out of its bottle and refusing to go back.

Just as concern about civilian power plants often distracted attention from the far graver matter of nuclear weapons, so the question of military secrecy surrounding genetic engineering tended to be overlooked in the debate. When the Public Opinion Laboratory of Northern Illinois University polled religious, environmental, and science policy leaders about attitudes to recombinant-DNA research, in 1984, only 5 percent mentioned weapons as a risk, compared with 69 percent who visualized the possible creation of undesirable organisms. Had the U.S. Air Force possessed forest-eating bacteria during the Vietnam War, would it have refrained from using them in preference to the 2,4,5-T defoliant, to clear the vegetation that concealed the Vietnamese enemies?

Pieces for Green Machines

Although genetic manipulation was the element in the new biotechnology that aroused most expectation and controversy, new possibilities for would-be engineers of green systems appeared from quite different directions—even overhead. The remote sensing satellites that detected visible and infrared radiation from the Earth's surface, or used radar to probe it, created a revolution in human ability to observe the state of vegetation, whether natural or planted. Especially when combined with computer models, as already managed by the weather forecasters, images from space promised to put environmental science and land-use planning on a firmer scientific basis.

Electronics at ground level provided an ever-wider and cheaper range of sensors for keeping an eye on the physical and chemical conditions of crops. These were gradually moving out of the laboratory into the commercial greenhouses and even into open fields. An ingenious example of new instrumentation for agriculture, from the Weizmann Institute in Israel, checked the efficiency of crops in their use of sunlight by pulsing light through optical fibers onto a small part of the leaf. They measured how much of the light was used by detecting the intensity of sound from a small chamber of carbon dioxide gas attached to the leaf.

Inexpensive equipment could make better use of resources in the web of living things. With microcomputers, farmers began monitoring the milk yields from every cow and allocating food of just the right amount and kind to each animal. This optimized the output in relation to the inputs and the state of the market, which could be more valuable for the farmer than a gross increase in the milk yields. Dutch agricultural engineers were to the fore in developing computer systems for dairy farming.

Wheat straw left after harvesting was a nuisance for farmers, who often burned it to clear their fields, to the great annoyance of neighbors. In Britain, the Agriculture and Food Research Council mobilized its laboratories to find ways of putting some 12 million tons of straw a year to better use. One lab grew mushrooms on the straw. Another reported that the carbon dioxide produced by rotting straw could be piped to greenhouses to improve yields; it also cultivated nitrogen-fixing bacteria on straw. And the council's agricultural engineers developed machinery for incorporating the straw back into the soil, deeply enough to avoid harming the seedlings of the next crop. But this was really a way of getting rid of the straw inoffensively, rather than exploiting it shrewdly; burning at least had the merit of controlling weeds and pests, and of returning some nutrients to the upper soil.

Other kinds of machinery unlocked disregarded resources, including leaf protein. Leaves from a few species (spinach, cabbage, lettuce) figured in the human diet, but all leaves were a potential source of protein—including conspicuously wasted leaves from crops like potatoes and sugar beets. In several countries, machines flailed and squeezed protein from fibrous leaves for feeding to pigs and poultry. N. W. Pirie, who pioneered the technique at Britain's Rothamsted Experimental Station, regretted that leaf protein was not used also for human food. He estimated that, in Britain, wasted leaves from potatoes, sugar beets, and vegetables could supply as much edible protein as all the country's beef herds.

The same Rothamsted lab spawned, in the 1980s, a company called British Earthworm Technology. It was devoted to harvesting earthworms from pits of animal waste, cleaning them, and converting them into a paste of dried and ground material for use in animal feeds. The earthworm of choice, *Eisenia foetida*, was a glutton for manure, and two-thirds of its dry weight consisted of high-grade protein. It was as good as fish or meat for feeding to pigs and poultry, and especially valuable for young turkeys. In Britain alone 100 million tons of animal manure not only went to waste, but created problems of disposal. Turning it into animal feed, via earthworms, was an interesting alternative to making biogas.

Using zeolites, porous minerals capable of absorbing water like a sponge, the Zeopower Company in Massachusetts devised a range of solar-powered refrigerators with no moving parts. The zeolite was sealed in a vacuum system. During the day, the heat of the sun evaporated water from the zeolite. In a condenser, the water vapor released its heat to the outside air or an external water-heating system. It then flowed as a cool liquid into a storage tank. At night the zeolite recharged itself with water vapor. Using this principle, the company devised walk-in coolers suitable for fishing villages and milk coolers for Third World dairies. On a hot, sunny day, a zeolite panel of 1.5 square meters could cool 60 liters of milk by 20° C.

High on the list of equipment for green machines were techniques for growing crops in artificial environments, as in the Italian work on growing *Spirulina* in transparent water pipes, in the growth chambers of the plant scientists, and in the demonstrations at the Disney Epcot Center in Florida. But the most familiar artificial environment was the greenhouse. In some people's imaginations a green machine should be a super-greenhouse.

In the seventeenth century, astonishing though it is to recall, Europeans did not realize that plants needed light to grow. When they raised pineapples and oranges in "hothouses" warmed with stoves, the rooms had ordinary windows. Fully developed greenhouses, with the maximum use of glass, did not become common until the mid-nineteenth century. They offered protection against the pests and weather, and could be heated in winter; sometimes they had to be cooled in the summer. The enclosure of the crops made feasible certain growing techniques that would be impracticable out-of-doors— for example, adding carbon dioxide to the air to make plants grow faster.

High operating costs, especially for heating, restricted the commercial use of conventional greenhouses to the production of tomatoes, lettuces, cucumbers, ornamental flowers, and a few other high-value crops. Farmers in China and Japan found it a good idea simply to cover open fields with plastic sheets. By the mid-1980s, huge areas in eastern Asia were benefiting from this simple protection against the worst of the climate. Another approach to cut-price shelters for crops was to make inflatable tents of transparent plastic, perhaps with a framework of inflatable struts.

Scientifically designed greenhouses were becoming quite sophisticated. "Solar" greenhouses used a minimum of energy by making the most of the sun's heat in winter. They often used steep, insulated roofs, dark-painted walls and water tanks to absorb and reradiate heat, and solar-driven ventilation systems. When Carla Mueller and her colleagues at Pennsylvania State University reported in 1977 on the performance of several designs for solar greenhouses, it became clear that the annual yields were poor. Cucumber production, even the most favorable case, was less than 10 percent of typical yields in conventional greenhouses. On the other hand, the results were still an improvement on outdoor farming, and by combining a solar greenhouse with living accommodations, as in Victorian conservatories, substantial savings in home heating were possible.

Particularly imaginative designs for greenhouses came from John Todd and his colleagues in the New Alchemy Institute, founded on Cape Cod, Massachusetts. They pioneered new lifestyles in bioshelters that integrated greenhouses with homes and fish farms. By 1982, the New Alchemists had developed the pillow dome: a geodesic greenhouse built of aluminum and windowed with triple membranes of transparent plastic. Argon gas sealed into these pillows acted as an insulator, cutting by 15 to 20 percent the escape of heat at night. In winter, a night curtain reduced the losses due to radiation. Buckminster Fuller, inventor of the geodesic dome, welcomed the integration of his architecture with biology.

The interior of the dome was a coherent system. "Solar ponds," actually freestanding cylindrical tanks of translucent fiberglass, took in light from all sides and carried dense masses of algae. They were populated by fish that obtained most of their food from the algae. The tanks absorbed the energy of sunlight during the day, released heat into the dome at night, and also supplied trickles of enriched irrigation water to the vegetable beds.

Apart from a favored fig tree (around which the dome was built) and an ornamental fish pond purified by water hyacinth, the rest of the growing area in the pillow dome was given over to vegetable beds in natural unsterilized soil. Using organic methods, the New Alchemists reported vegetable yields three times higher than the averages quoted by the U.S. Department of Agriculture, while the production of fish in their solar tanks sometimes matched the world records for aquaculture. A computer monitored the state of the building as if it were a hospital patient in intensive care.

Looking to the future, Nancy Jack Todd and John Todd visualized an end to the segregation of food production from community life. In a city subdivided into self-organizing villages, food from greenhouses and gardens would be sold directly to the local consumers, without the usual packaging or transportation. They described a village arranged like the spokes of a wheel around a central lake, and built of solid materials and transparent membranes, as a single structure with varying degrees of exposure to the sky. The wedges devoted to agriculture might be open to the sky in summer and covered by transparent tents in winter.

Buckminster Fuller had described a geodesic dome to cover New York City that would keep the city warm in winter and cool in the summer. In the 1980s, European engineers designed a greenhouse town for the Canadian government, which was planning to create a settlement for 12,000 people near Fort McMurray, in the chilly wilderness of northern Alberta. Frei Otto of Germany, who designed the Olympic stadium in Munich, joined forces with the British firm Buro Happold to conceive a town covering 14 hectares and enclosed by a transparent dome 60 meters high. The dome was to be made of fluorocarbon film with an expected life of forty years. It would be supported, not by a rigid frame, but a slight excess of air pressure, maintained by fans. The falling price of oil caused the Canadian government to shelve its plans for exploiting the oil sands of Alberta, but the detailed engineering, architectural, and sociological studies had established principles that could be applied anywhere in the world.

While John Todd stressed the virtues of natural soil, Allen Cooper grew crops without any soil at all. The nutrient-film technique, which he developed in England by 1973, bathed the roots of the plants in a stream of nutrient-rich water trickling down a channel made, for example, of plastic or concrete. The roots happily splayed and matted themselves in the channel; the nutrients they extracted were replenished before the water was recirculated to bathe the roots again. Thus was born the first truly economical mode of hydroponics, a long-standing idea of cultivating large, nonaquatic plants in water.

Against those who regarded the soil as the very embodiment of Mother Earth and the only fit environment for the roots of crops, enthusiasts for the nutrient-film technique pointed out that natural soil was the source of most of the pests and diseases that afflicted plants. They also noted the terrible damage being done to the soil, as conventional agriculture strove to feed the world. Cooper foresaw that the technique would raise crops in all kinds of soilless environments: on the roofs and walls of buildings, on mountainsides, or out in space. Properly managed, the nutrient water could be supplied from biological rather than chemical sources.

The chief thing to be said in favor of soil was that it was more forgiving of human blunders than the nutrient-film technique, where a single mistake could kill the crops. Early applications of the system were by skilled greenhouse operators, using elaborate monitoring and automatic-control techniques. When Cooper joined forces with Kenneth Edwards of Ariel Industries, who shared his interest in hydroponic systems and their possible application in the Third World, they devised simpler operating procedures, with most of the work being done by hand. A small service center could carry out the laboratory work for the operators of hundreds of hectares of nutrient-film production, supplying them with sachets of nutrients for the following week, formulated by computer in the light of information about the state of the crop in the previous week. Edwards and Cooper tested their procedures among growers in southern Spain.

In the "Second Generation NFT" the configuration of the feeding channels changed. Roots needed to be able to breathe as well as imbibe, and the experimenters divided the roots of each plant between two channels. The nutrient solution could then fully immerse the roots, but only in one channel at a time, leaving the other roots exposed to the air. One of the first benefits to appear with this arrangement was that the plants better withstood and exploited intense light. A further discovery was that short bursts of greatly enriched nutrients could in effect force-feed the crops and make them grow faster. In an early experiment with cucumbers, Cooper reported an increase of more than 50 percent in the yield of fruit.

As a precaution against interruptions of the supply of food and water, damp capillary matting covered the divided gullies and dipped into the return channel that carried the nutrient solution for recycling. Trials showed that plants would grow quite well even if they received shots of fresh nutrient only once an hour. So the nutrient-film technique would work even among people who lacked the power supplies to drive the small pumps that usually circulated the solution continuously.

For applications in industrialized countries, Edwards and

Cooper found that they could control the flavor of tomatoes grown by the nutrient-film technique, by adjusting the level of sugar supplied to the plants. Even the tomatoes grown in the course of experiments had such excellent flavor that a supermarket chain asked, unsolicited, for a continuous supply to be sold at premium prices. So much for the belief that "natural" methods of production produced the best-tasting food.

Although a superstitious belief in the superiority of low-tech methods of food production was unwarranted, these methods often demonstrated important benefits of biodynamic feedback in green systems. John Jeavons at Palo Alto, for example, reported extremely high yields from careful gardening with no nonbiological inputs. The coexistence of "natural" and "engineered" techniques among new-style gardeners was a matter for satisfaction rather than ideological conflict. Quite different approaches could offer increased food production from smaller areas of land, while conserving the soil. The two approaches could be blended by building nutrient-film channels from bamboo and obtaining the nutrient solutions from "natural" sources, as Allen Cooper himself pointed out. The most important benefit was that communities creating green machines would be able to choose for themselves the technologies they favored, instead of being forced to follow industrial or political fashions.

Greener Than Green

Nature painted the landscapes with deep green microdots in every cell of every leaf. The chloroplasts were egg-shaped objects so small that two hundred of them end to end would barely stretch a millimeter. As self-contained units, they performed the most important task on Earth: photosynthesis. They trapped the radiant energy from the sun and converted it into chemical forms that their plant hosts could handle.

The chloroplasts were bacteria that more than a billion years in the past took up permanent residence in larger and more complicated living cells. They paid generous rent for their lodgings by conferring the power to eat daylight. They retained

106 THE GREEN MACHINES

a great deal of independence, with bacterialike genes within the chloroplasts themselves supplying most of their own needs; these genes were passed on directly to daughter chloroplasts in new plant cells.

The wondrous molecular machinery for snapping up passing particles of light and turning them into chemical energy evolved among bacteria very early in the history of life on Earth. In a tour de force of molecular analysis, Johann Deisenhofer and his colleagues at the Max Planck Institute for Biochemistry near Munich discovered the complete arrangement of the photosynthetic reaction center of a purple bacterium, *Rhodopseudomonas viridis.* It turned out to be an intricate framework of four large protein molecules fitted out with several pigment molecules—not the usual chlorophyll pigment of green plants but a bacterial equivalent. When one end of the assembly of pigments caught a photon of light, an electron bounced through the molecules like a ball in a pinball machine. At the far end it chemically altered a mobile molecule of quinone, which thereupon departed with a cargo of chemical energy to set in train a series of further chemical reactions.

The bacterial ancestors of the chloroplasts altered the Earth's atmosphere, changing it from a gas rich in carbon dioxide to a gas rich in oxygen. They went on in the same vein. In essence, they split water into its constituents. They released the oxygen and used the hydrogen to convert carbon dioxide into the carbon-based components needed for life. Overall, the chief reactions of photosynthesis required six molecules of water and six of carbon dioxide, together with the energy of nine or ten photons, to produce one molecule of glucose and six molecules of oxygen. Further photosynthetic reactions took in nitrogen, phosphorus, sulfur and other nutrients to make more complicated compounds—proteins, for example.

Contrary to a widespread conviction that "Nature knows best," plants were the wrong color to exploit the daylight to their fullest advantage. To do so, they should have evolved to be the same gray or black color as photovoltaic silicon cells. The green that soothed the eyes amid rural scenery was wasted energy—valuable photons of green light rejected by the plants. In theory it might be possible to engineer blacker plants by incorporating into the cells of the leaves other bacteria that used green and infrared light.

If green machines were to remain literally green, much depended on making the most of the existing chloroplasts. They used the absorbed red and blue light quite well. Their gross efficiency in converting photons into the chemical energy of "fixed" carbon was about 30 percent. Many factors whittled away at that energy. A wide range of crop plants became saturated long before sunlight reached its full intensity, and so were not able to use all the available energy. Local shortages of carbon dioxide were created externally by lack of wind and internally by bottlenecks in the pores through which the leaves breathed. These impeded the process of photosynthesis, and only a few plants (pineapple was one) had the good sense to stockpile carbon dioxide at night.

Even in ideal conditions, with ample water and nutrients, crop plants converted only 3 or 4 percent of the radiant energy of sunlight into growth in their durable fabric. Bare ground was the most visible reason why typical yields on farms fell far below even this modest percentage. For maximum use of the sun's energy it was obviously necessary to keep leaves spread over every square centimeter of land, at all seasons. On the other hand, in densely growing vegetation most leaves were shaded by other leaves, so the energy used to grow the leaves was largely wasted. From that point of view, the ideal crop would have flat leaves like a water lily's.

Plants used up most of the absorbed energy just in keeping themselves alive. This was necessary in principle, but in practice much of the energy was needlessly lost or squandered. Genetic engineers saw room for improvement. Indeed it would be surprising if a casual union between a green bacterium and another cell resulted in the best possible chemistry for human farming some 1300 million years later, when the world was very different and carbon dioxide was in short supply. Certain reactions in the chloroplasts and leaves limited the rate of photosynthesis or else channeled the energy into wasteful processes. By suppressing parasitical enzymes and reinforcing the most beneficial ones, manipulation might make photosynthesis more efficient and plant growth more vigorous.

The life of a plant was governed by light. It influenced the activity of at least twenty genes, so governing many different functions from the manufacture of chlorophyll to the plant's decision that the days had become long enough for it to flower. Genetic engineers hoped to find many handles for adjusting the plant's response to light. One light-sensitive gene carried instructions for making the enzyme that grabbed carbon-dioxide molecules for incorporation in the photosynthetic process. In 1984 two groups announced the successful transfer of this gene from peas into other plants. A Monsanto–Rockefeller University team put it into petunias, the Ghent–Max Planck team, into tobacco. In both cases the gene functioned normally in its new environment and switched off in the dark. These were the first tentative steps toward teaching plants how to do better in their work of growing by sunlight.

Were plants obsolete as the preferred way of converting energy of sunlight into chemical forms that human beings could eat and use in other ways? Those who favored growing small algae in water could claim to be dispensing with the redundancies of leaves and roots. Going a stage further, experimenters took the chloroplasts out of spinach, boosted them with an added enzyme and other chemicals, exposed them to light, and produced hydrogen gas. In other words they had split water. A further step down the road of simplification would be to take pieces of the photosynthetic membrane from bacterial cells and use those to generate an electric current.

To chemists, even isolated chloroplasts or their membranes seemed unnecessarily complicated molecular apparatus for performing the chemical task of using daylight to split water. It was like building a Mercedes just to be able to set fire to gasoline. Two Nobel-prize chemists, Sir George Porter in London and Melvin Calvin in Berkeley, California, were prominent in a drive by photochemists to try to improve on natural photosynthesis. They demonstrated several possible reactions that liberated hydrogen from water, or incorporated the hydrogen in a chemical compound.

An obvious use for the liberated hydrogen or a modified molecule was to recombine it with oxygen in fuel cells to generate electricity. Groups at Canterbury and Oxford experimented with enzymes to improve on the conventional fuel cell. More generally, the hydrogen might supply a "hydrogen economy." In this, hydrogen distributed through pipes, or carried bound to metals, might serve as the predominant fuel for industrial and domestic use, and for propelling cars and rocket planes. Hydrogen could also be the starting point for making food artificially in factories, without any further need for sunlight. Enthusiastic chemists could visualize many enticing combinations of chemical synthesis, microbe and animal rearing, and the growing of plants by artificial light.

In the mid-1980s, the chloroplast manipulators and the chemists who started from scratch were upstaged by the semiconductor physicists who developed a new generation of cheap and efficient photovoltaic cells, using amorphous silicon. They generated electricity directly from sunlight, and if a hydrogen economy were still the objective, the power would split water by conventional electrolysis. This process was 70 percent efficient in the use of electrical energy, while photovoltaic cells were expected to be at least 10 percent efficient in converting daylight into electricity.

Here were figures that gave all plant breeders, genetic engineers, algae cultivators, and photochemists a clear target to beat if they could. They had to try to use the available energy from the sun to produce hydrogen or hydrogen-rich compounds with an efficiency of better than 7 percent. That meant a system fourteen times more efficient in photosynthesis than the average American cornfield. By 1986, Porter the chemist was himself saying "back to the chloroplast." Advances in biotechnology were opening new ways of meeting the challenge of the gray engineers and achieving efficiencies in photosynthesis far surpassing anything accomplished before.

101 Things to Do with a Tennis Court

Among all the reasons for chasing efficiency in the use of sunlight to levels far surpassing those achieved in conventional agriculture, the simplest was necessity. Figures from the World

Bank and the UN Food and Agriculture Organization, projecting population trends and the use of land, made it that clear that the time when agronomists could think in hectares or acres was ending. In future it would be a matter of square meters. By the mid twenty-first century, people in Nigeria, Indonesia, China, and other parts of Africa and Asia would have to be fed from shares of arable land that worked out at 350 to 400 square meters for each member of the populations. In Bangladesh, where human numbers were expected to quadruple between 1980 and 2050, the arable land per head would be down to 250 square meters. That was slightly less than the 261 square meters (about 2800 square feet) of the marked playing area of a doubles tennis court.

To enable Bangladeshis and others to feed themselves well from a tennis court per head was an achievable goal. That being so, people in other parts of the world could think in similar terms, as a matter of convenience. If food could be produced from much smaller areas, and major contributions to human needs for energy and materials also came from highly efficient solar and biological sources, people could live closer to these sources. Elaborate systems of storage, processing and distribution could be simplified. This was the practical nub of the ideas about decentralization and self-reliance in human social systems.

In the end it was a matter of numbers, and of what green machines might produce from a given area of land. In systems based on living plants, the overall efficiency of photosynthesis was a key factor. Solar and agronomic experts used many different systems of reckoning, potentially confusing for them and for everyone else. Quite apart from the diverse measuring units used, one person might specify the total annual solar radiation received, while another cited the direct sunlight, or the radiation falling on crops during the growing season. Output might be given in terms of gross weight, dry weight, or energy of combustion. Care was needed to compare like with like. Further complications arose from the geographical variations in available solar radiation, not to mention the ecological differences and the variable performance of crops in different environments. Asking what you could do with a tennis court was a useful way of bringing the technical and arithmetical questions to a focus.

The arable land available to the world as a whole in 1980 was equivalent on average to more than twelve tennis courts per person (3300 square meters). The World Bank, in its 1984 projection, expected the world's population to grow from 4435 million in 1980 to about 9800 million by the year 2050, with the rate of increase easing markedly by then. Assuming a 20 percent loss of arable land, 4.7 tennis courts' worth would be left for each person in 2050.

From country to country, there were huge variations. In Japan, in 1981, the arable land per head was already less than two tennis courts (400 square meters), while the average American's share of the arable land worked out at about twenty tennis courts (5600 square meters). In countries more typical than either Japan or the U.S., five tennis courts' worth of arable land per person was an approximate figure for the Netherlands and the Federal Republic of Germany, and seven or eight for Italy, Nigeria, and Kenya. In African countries, population growth was pulling the numbers down very rapidly.

If the tennis court per head were treated as an achievable target for the mid twenty-first century, other general arithmetic flowed from it. The whole human population, after more than doubling, could be fed from about a quarter of the arable land in use in the 1980s. In countries with land to spare, people would allow themselves more elbow room in their buildings and towns, but much of the land would be freed for other purposes and for returning to Nature, either as tamed parkland or as reengineered wilderness. Those visualizing decentralized communities would calculate in terms of a tennis court per head for food production. Adding a second tennis court per person, to allow for homes and gardens, public buildings, factories, roads, and so on, would make a community of 10,000 people about 500 hectares in area, or a circle of territory about 2.6 kilometers (1.6 miles) in diameter. But then the question arose: How much of their energy and materials, as well as food, could they produce for themselves?

To speak in terms of arable land begged various questions

about the character of the green machines. Only 10 percent of the world's total land surface was cultivated. The rest of the land, where it had not simply been built upon, was judged too cold, too dry, too wet, too steep, or otherwise too poor for cultivation by ordinary methods. On the other hand, grazing land and also the rivers, lakes, and oceans, were left out of the reckoning, and they would remain important sources of food. For those who thought of growing crops in urban areas by the nutrient-film technique, or plastering photovoltaic cells on arid crags to bring the desert to life, obstacles to conventional farming often seemed like opportunities. But the arable land remained the best land, either to be used frugally for human purposes, or to be handed back to Nature. Relating the possibilities to present and foreseeable needs for arable land also linked green machines of the imagination to the real world of farming.

One more caveat to avoid misunderstanding: In considering the 101 things that might be done with a plot of land the size of a tennis court, the idea was not that each individual should manage his own small plot. It would obviously be comical to try to produce pigs and electricity and all the other forms of food, materials, and energy supplies, from handkerchief-sized portions of private property. A community using green machines would group the various crops and functions in much larger segments of the total land available to it. The arithmetic of the tennis court was meant simply to keep problems and goals in the simplest perspective by taking account of what each individual could reasonably claim as his share of the land and its sunshine.

A useful round number to conjure with was a typical figure for the radiant energy from the sun (direct and indirect) falling on each square meter of the land surface. It was 1 million kilocalories per year, totaled over the seasons. (A kilocalorie was, confusingly, the same as the "large calorie" used by dieticians and weight watchers.) This worked out at an average of 2740 kilocalories per square meter per day, and by coincidence, it was about the same as the energy from food needed by the average individual each day. In other words, if sunlight could be converted into food with 100 percent efficiency, each

person could eat the produce from just 1 square meter of land
and use the rest for playing tennis.

In practice, of course, yields would be far lower. The areas
of the alleys ("tramlines") on the two sides of a tennis court,
used in doubles matches, occupied 64 square meters. If these
were allocated to food production, a year-round photosynthetic
efficiency of 1.56 percent would fulfill the needs for a vegeta-
rian diet. Biodynamic gardeners might claim to be able to reach
such a figure, though perhaps at the cost of considerable manual
labor. Farmers following the best practices of advanced farming technology could also achieve that photosynthetic efficiency, though with hidden inputs of energy from sources other
than the sun.

In any case most people would still want to eat meat, milk,
eggs, and so on. To supply the necessary animal feed would
greatly increase the kilocalorie requirements. The livestock
would need space as well, and depending on local attitudes
to intensive animal-rearing methods, this could vary widely.
The simplest guide to the land requirement for a generous
diet came from the rich countries of the 1980s, where more
than three times as much land was used for keeping and feeding
animals as for producing cereals and vegetables for direct
human consumption. On this basis, the whole of the tennis
court would be taken up with food production. Everyone
would be eating well—perhaps too well—but there would
be nothing left over for the production of materials and energy except other land spared by the intensive production of
food.

Expectations of future energy requirements were the wildest
guesswork. Energy forecasters in industrialized countries, who
had been predicting exponential growth in demand, had to
make a U-turn and to contemplate falling demand, as energy-
saving measures began to bite. And anyone visualizing self-
reliant communities was hard put to it to figure out the relationship between new lifestyles and energy consumption. Certainly
there could be great savings in the energy for transport and
heating, and in low-temperature methods of manufacture by
bio-industries. On the other hand, uses for energy, for example
in watering the deserts and producing materials by chemical

or biochemical synthesis, deserved to be increased. "Back-to-Nature" scenarios often sought to minimize energy use, and the idea that the world's poor countries might aspire to energy intensities like those of the industrialized world was often treated as if it were farfetched. It was even more farfetched, though, to imagine that the greater part of the human species would tolerate permanent impoverishment in respect of energy.

The consumption of commercial energy in Japan in the 1980s was the equivalent of 30 million kilocalories per person per year. This was less than half the consumption of the average American, but seventeen times the average Indian's. The world average consumption was a rather meaningless figure, in view of the differences between rich and poor countries, but it worked out at about 16 million kilocalories per year. All things considered, the Japanese figure of 30 million kilocalories might be a sensible norm for the mid twenty-first century. This would require a quadrupling of energy supplies worldwide, taking account of the increase in population.

To produce 30 million kilocalories per person per year by photovoltaic cells, with an expected conversion efficiency of 10 percent, would need 300 square meters. Biological methods of energy conversion would be hard pressed to match that performance, never mind improve on it. It was salutary for solar-energy enthusiasts to see that their demands for land could easily outstrip those needed for food production by advanced methods.

There was no point in being purist or prescriptive about using energy supplies from the sun, or ignoring the many other sources of energy. Even if the oil ran out, a great deal of coal remained—although that might best be regarded as a chemical feedstock for the future. If nuclear energy was still to be taken seriously, after a Ukrainian plant exploded, submarine reactors remained a model for anyone wanting to visualize decentralized power production, perhaps safer in local hands than in secretive large-scale nuclear industries.

Much of the world's hydroelectricity and tidal power was still untapped, wave power had yet to be tried, and there were hopes of recovering energy latent in the underground heat that occurred everywhere in the world. Tree cropping from managed forests could be treated as another bonus, not to be debited to the tennis court. Windmills, driven by air set in motion by the sun's heat, could be regarded as a whirly form of solar power plant.

Some of these energy sources, particularly coal mines and waterfalls, were by their nature concentrated and localized and might best be used for specialized purposes such as metal smelting and major irrigation schemes. The others represented a wide range of options about which no opinions need be expressed. The idea that people in future would run their own lives in decentralized communities prohibited its advocates from prescribing or ruling out particular technologies. The task was to show that prosperous self-reliant communities were possible, one way or another.

Taking the worst case, a community with access to no special sources could meet perhaps half the supposed energy needs by covering with solar collectors the roofs and walls of buildings in areas allocated for human occupancy, although this could very well interfere with other ideas for using sunlight in buildings. The cultivated areas would generate waste material and manure that could be turned into biogas or other energetic products. The feedbacks between energy inputs and energy outputs, and recycling within the system, were too complex for casual analysis, but at best these sources could meet only a few percent of the energy needs. The price would be a loss of materials for soil fertilization, animal feed, or chemical manufacture. To supply by other means the missing 15 million kilocalories of energy per head per year, for a community of 10,000 people, would not be particularly difficult, as it corresponded with an electrical power supply of 20 megawatts—very modest by the standards of modern power stations. Windmills of advanced design might cost several thousand dollars per person to install. Diesel-electric generators would probably be cheaper, but then more land would be taken up, if energy crops were to provide the fuel.

Materials production might come in conventional forms like cotton, or as biological feedstock for chemical manufacture. The worldwide production of cotton, jute, and natural rubber, the chief plant products, amounted to about 5 kilograms per person per year in the 1980s. Far greater was the production of synthetic organic materials, which in the U.S. was running at 350 kilograms per American per year around 1980. Growing 350 kilograms of biomass as a chemical feedstock might require almost half a tennis court, and self-reliant communities wanting to replace metal with plastic could need much more than that.

These reckonings assumed systems that were highly efficient though attainable by the agricultural science and conventional biotechnology of the 1980s, with about 1.5 percent conversion of energy by photosynthesis. They would represent a big improvement on Nature, whose overall efficiency of photosynthesis on land was less than 0.3 percent; an advance, too, over average American farming practices circa 1980, which achieved 0.5 percent in corn production. But 1.5 percent efficiency fell short of what was needed if Bangladeshis were to do more than feed themselves and if compact communities elsewhere were to be thoroughly self-reliant without either accepting a fall in living standards or resuming the pressure on available land. By the technologies of the 1980s, a tennis court was not enough to supply food, energy, and materials.

Even for the classic problem of feeding the world, everything looked uncomfortably tight, if one remembered the estimate of 4.7 tennis courts of arable land per head by 2050. As long as there was room for serious doubts about the ability of farmers to produce enough nourishment for their multiplying compatriots, a sense of emergency was bound to infect policies. People were unlikely to feel free to reconsider how they wanted to live, let alone to do so in a wise and imaginative frame of mind. The drive for productivity in the green revolution of the 1960s and 1970s harmed the spirit of community in rural areas. It created new inequities between employers and employees among the farmers, and between men and women. It also swept aside traditional concerns for soil conservation and the living environment.

Farmers in the swamplands of southern Borneo, ordered by the Indonesian government to grow green-revolution rice, soon

gave up and converted their rice fields into coconut plant-
ings and fish ponds. In reporting this minor agronomic rebellion, Gordon Conway, an environmental technologist at
Imperial College, London, said it was easy to see why.
The coconuts grew better, suffered far less from pests and
the acid soil, and earned a steady income for the farmers
without the erratic fluctuations in price from which rice suffered. Any family could grow the coconuts, without hiring labor for planting and harvesting. The people preferred sta-
bility and equitability with a somewhat less productive crop
to the pursuit of the highest possible yields regardless of social costs.

The ill-effects of the green revolution were liable to repeat
and multiply during the next phase of the race against hunger,
as the land per mouth shrank in large areas of the world. To
check them would require a conscious effort to defend the
rights of farming people and to integrate food production more
carefully with the local environment. The task for the new
biotechnology was not to produce narrow-minded high-tech
solutions to be imposed by foreign-trained experts on "back-
ward" people, but to multiply the people's options. Forgotten
arts of mixed farming and crop rotation ranked high among
the things that could be done with limited land—now with
the warranties of computerized system analyses, as at Injambakkam. At the same time, biotechnologists had to use their
special skills to increase yields sufficiently to allow everyone
to catch their breath.

These were reasons for stressing the importance of the new
biotechnology for human life. The generosity of sunlight was
tantalizing. In energy content it was equivalent to more than
100 liters of gasoline raining on each square meter of ground
in the course of a year. If the technologies could be brought
together to boost photosynthetic efficiency in highly nourishing
crops, to fix nitrogen by better means, to grow fibers and animal
products in underground vats, to exploit solar ponds, and to
control the environment of leaves and roots in greenhouses
and nutrient-film channels, the tennis court would feel much
less claustrophobic. If the net result were to supply a good
nonvegetarian diet from half the area, leaving the rest of the

tennis court for raising a few tons of biomass or biofuels using artificially enhanced photosynthesis, the prospects would be brighter. By making better use of the powers of light, the new biotechnology would move the concept of the green machines forward, from a desperate effort to cope, toward the promise of a more relaxed, affluent, and generous world.

3 POWERS OF DARKNESS

As long as the human world was in a reliable state, futurologists could anticipate technology to come by consulting knowledgeable and imaginative scientists and engineers in various fields and asking them what long-term possibilities they saw arising from their work. In the period 1945 to 1985 that method gave quite good predictions twenty years into the future, which was roughly how long it took for a major new idea to be developed to the point where it had a noticeable impact on human affairs. Other matters besides technology could be predicted over a similar timespan. But any success in forecasting of that kind depended on stable conditions in human society, such that minor technical and social changes could pile up like sediments settling on a firm seabed.

If volcanic changes were pending, and the accumulation of technological skills confronted people with fateful choices and far-reaching alterations in society, estimates of progress in, say, rail transport or cancer therapy, were footling by comparison. A quite different method of forecasting the future of technology was then more appropriate. This paid less attention to the details of current technology, and more to the fundamental possibilities and limits set by physics and biology; also more attention to basic human needs, desires, and urges, whether good or bad. It asked what would happen if people went down such and such a road as far as it could lead. The writer H. G. Wells was one of the pioneers of "going to extremes."

In 1885, at the age of nineteen, Wells stood up in the debating society of the Normal School of Science in South Kensington and described the future of the human race. On the basis of certain trends in human evolution, he visualized people large of brain and slight of body, with unnecessary appendages like hair and eyebrows evolved away, while teeth, stomach and the other organs of digestion would be replaced with a system of feeding through the skin, by immersion in a tub of nutritive fluid. These "earthly cherubim" or "human tadpoles," as Wells called them, would be alone on the planet. Having discovered the secret of how "to do the work of chlorophyll without the plant," and to win food from dead rocks and the sunlight, "the man of the year million" would dispense with all plants and animals. They would succumb to his "inventiveness" and "discipline." In making this prediction, Wells did not mean to commend such an outcome. He remarked, rather pompously for a young student, "The contemplative man shivers at the prospect."

Prophecy of this kind was always open to mockery. In 1904, two years after Wells had published his juvenile fantasy and other anticipations in book form, his fellow writer G. K. Chesterton poked fun at all extrapolators by quoting an imaginary Dr. Pellkins:

> . . . just as we know, when we see weeds and dandelions growing more and more thickly in a garden, that they must, in spite of all our efforts, grow taller than the chimney-pots and swallow the house from sight, so we know and reverently acknowledge, that when any power in human politics has shown for any period of time any considerable activity, it will go on until it reaches to the sky.

Chesterton commended a game played by the human race, called "Cheat the Prophet."

> The players listen very carefully and respectfully to all that the clever men have to say about what is to happen in the next generation. The players then wait until all the clever men are dead, and bury them nicely. They then go and do something else.

The Napoleon of Notting Hill, from which these quotations come, remained required reading for anyone presumptuous enough to speculate about the future; also for those interested in a comic scenario for political decentralization in an urban setting. Nevertheless, one Wellsian proposition that Chesterton mocked was the idea that there might be forms of transport swifter than the motorcar. Regardless of the fallibility of prophets, technology was in reality changing Chesterton's world at an accelerating pace. Unrepentant scientists, including J. B. S.

Haldane and J. D. Bernal, continued to "go to extremes" as a useful way of caricaturing the tendencies in technology and making them easier to grasp and reason about. By the 1970s and 1980s, their mantle had fallen on Freeman Dyson, a Princeton physicist and the most imaginative scientist of his time.

Bernal, for example, went beyond the atrophied human beings visualized by Wells to describe Disembodied Brains, coupled to sensors, manipulators, and life-support systems. That was in 1929. Although the idea was distasteful to many, including its author, a fair-minded observer might say that many of the tendencies in medical science during the following half century—in surgery, prosthetic devices, and intensive care— drove strongly in that direction. Even by the 1980s, no one had any clear idea about how a Disembodied Brain might be wired up, especially to receive the sensory inputs without which it would quickly go mad. But it remained a conceivable end product of medical research, appealing perhaps to rich people craving immortality.

For those desiring slaves and an escape from childbearing, the Baby Factory pictured by the novelist Aldous Huxley in *Brave New World* (1932) was another case of "going to extremes." The methods of growing fetuses in bottles and retarding their mental development described in the novel were an imaginative extension of techniques in embryology that were emerging in primitive forms when Huxley wrote his book. Again, manipulations in the subsequent decades forged ahead in the direction visualized by Huxley. The experimenters who grew the first test-tube babies in the wombs of their mothers or surrogate mothers vehemently denied, to a public sensitized by Huxley's book, any dreams of a Baby Factory. The vision remained valid, if only as a warning.

By 1984, Aldous Huxley's son Matthew was giving another warning: that future governments might try to keep the growing numbers of unemployed people in a state of docility by giving them free access to safe psychedelic drugs in "drug pubs." This was in keeping with a vision that Freeman Dyson attributed to Francis Crick of DNA fame: the Cheap Thrills Machine. By electrical or more probably psychochemical stimulation of the brain, people could be given strong feelings of satisfaction if they behaved properly. Park your car legally and be rewarded with emotions comparable with those following a safe landing on Mars.

Irrespective of its precise technology or purpose, the Cheap Thrills Machine cartooned all the possibilities latent in medical science for manipulating human conduct and moods, as foreshadowed in the control of behavior in monkeys by remotely controlled electrodes implanted in their brains, and the successful treatment of psychiatric symptoms by drugs. The use of tear gas and other chemical agents for crowd control, the rising tide of self-administered drugs, and the psychochemical-drug regimes meted out to political dissidents in Soviet mental hospitals were crude precursors of the Cheap Thrills Machine.

These various machines and devices represented a style of thinking by which thoughtful commentators could advertise, or warn against, major trends in technology. Their value to prognosticators and their audiences was that they summed up in easily memorable phrases huge areas of human intellectual and practical endeavor that otherwise seemed impossibly complex to comprehend and vague in their consequences. A dozen or twenty of such putative devices could identify most of the trends in technology that raised important long-term issues of policy.

Their reflection of human needs, desires, and ambitions added force and plausibility to the concepts. Translating modern technology into extreme forms, in parable fashion, highlighted ancient issues about goals and fears, and right and wrong. Although they pitched their thoughts into the twenty-first century or beyond, the "imagineers" raised timely questions about twentieth-century policies. And the machines they visualized were not always as unambiguously repellent as in these first few examples.

A Choice of Cornucopias

Trends in manufacturing using robots and computers were summed up in the Santa Claus Machine. This was a device for eating rocks and making anything that human beings might desire, whether coffee cups, word processors, automobiles, spaceships or other Santa Claus Machines. Theodore Taylor, the American engineer who named the Santa Claus Machine, put an engineering gloss on the idea. You could atomize the rocks to separate all the chemical elements and recombine them to make any kind of material you fancied—metal alloys, plastics, ceramics, dyes, drugs—all to be worked into final products by robot-controlled tools and processing systems. The machinery might run on some combination of solar and nuclear energy, but the technical details were not very important. What mattered was that the Santa Claus Machine was conceivable. The principle had been laid down in 1947 (though not under this name) by the computer pioneer John Von Neumann, and subsequent technology moved in that direction.

Being organized with software very like that of a living organism, the Santa Claus Machine would be a self-providing and self-repairing system. If one simply added food production to the tasks allotted to the Santa Claus Machine, H. G. Wells's shiver-inducing vision of human beings dispensing altogether with the Earth's plants and animals might come to pass. But there would be no need to kill them off; on the contrary, it might do a lot of good for the other species of the planet if human beings no longer imposed on them for the provision of food, fiber, and energy. If there were objections to eating up the Rocky Mountains or the Sahara Desert, the Santa Claus Machine could be programmed to prettify its own waste dumps. Leaving such environmental issues aside, the parable of the Santa Claus Machine raised sharp political questions about industrial trends in the late twentieth century.

Seen optimistically, the Santa Claus Machine promised to relieve mankind of the drudgery of work in manufacturing industry. Putting that more negatively, it would make the manufacturing work force entirely redundant. As a great destroyer of jobs, the Santa Claus Machine caricatured the strains already evident in industrial societies in the age of automation. It also raised extraordinary questions about ownership, authority, and wealth.

Would the designer of the Santa Claus Machine be king? Or the entrepreneur who paid for its development? If neither of these, why not? If human labor lost all its material value, and at the same time anyone could ask the Santa Claus Machine for a Porsche, who would be able to say, and with what justification, that one person might have the car and another might not? How in short, would industrial civilization reorganize itself and its systems of rewards, if workers, managers, and entrepreneurs lost all function in the productive process? Biotechnological systems designed to run without human involvement, using automated control and manufacturing systems with auxiliary robots and other machinery, would raise the same starkly political questions.

The Green Machines (here with capital letters to assert their status as an "extreme" vision) were rivals of the Santa Claus Machines. They promised a similar cornucopia of products, but by a quite different route. While the Santa Claus Machine would be the culmination of gray machinery, the Green Machines would largely supersede it. So far from reducing everything to its atoms and operating at high temperatures, they were to make the maximum use of preexisting living systems and invented analogs, all running at low temperatures. That was their most revolutionary quality, and it would be a secondary matter for human beings to choose whether to operate the green systems themselves, or leave them in the charge of computers or biological control systems.

In a race between biotechnologists and robot engineers, between Green Machines and Santa Claus Machines, there were reasons why the Green Machines might win. Making a Santa Claus Machine would be a huge and costly enterprise, whereas Green Machines could operate usefully on a very small scale down to a flowerpot. Starting with food, Green Machines addressed urgent human needs. On the other hand, there was no point in being fastidious about gray versus green; a sensibly conceived Santa Claus Machine would use air and water in a plantlike fashion, while pumps made of steel and control systems made of silicon might be needed by green engineers far into the future. The outcome might be a hybrid rock-eater and sunlight-grower—a Green Santa Claus Machine.

Human beings of the late twentieth century could count themselves fortunate that they had a choice of technological routes to meeting all their productive needs in the future. Further promises of plenty were summed up in the vision of Space Cities. As with other extreme possibilities, this concept envisaged by J. D. Bernal, Freeman Dyson, Gerard O'Neill, and others, was based on the fundamentals of physics and biology. In this case, the starting point was the fact that only a very small fraction of the sun's rays fell on the Earth, and the idea was to tap the enormous quantities of solar energy running to waste out in space. For operating on a large scale away from home, materials would be more easily gathered from the smaller bodies of the solar system, such as the moon and asteroids, than from the Earth.

The space prophets visualized large revolving spheres in which people would live, grow their crops, and meet virtually all their needs from the space environment. In its physical economy, the Space City would be in effect a sophisticated Green Machine built by primitive Santa Claus Machines. People would spend their entire lives in space and visit the Earth only as tourists, but no shortage of volunteers was expected. The human species could multiply its numbers without limits out in space, packing first the solar system to capacity and then moving out to the environments of other stars. Expanding their territory at an average speed of 1 percent of the speed of light, subspecies of mankind could take possession of the entire Milky Way galaxy in a period of about ten million years.

Thinking about Space Cities fed back into the thinking about the future of the Earth. It was a remedy for a meanness of spirit induced by apparent overcrowding on a small planet, and it put events on the Earth in a salutary perspective. Political bickering ought not to be allowed to block a grand and adventurous phase of human existence, either by nuclear war on Earth or an arms race in the solar system. And if human beings could look forward to high living standards amid the sparse material resources of space, why should there be the slightest difficulty about doing well on the bountiful mother planet?

Technical possibilities of the kind visualized for space were far easier to handle on the Earth's surface, and there were great resources that no one had yet tried to exploit seriously. The Ocean City was a speculation that illustrated the possibili-

ties: a habitable machine, first cousin to a Space City, but floating pleasantly on the surface of a tropical ocean. A very deep
hull or other underwater structures would keep it stable, and
thus avoid seasickness among the inhabitants. A possible key
to the physics and biology was the sucking up of cold water
lying deep beneath the warm surface and doing two great
things with it. The first would be to generate energy from
the difference in temperature between the cold water and
the warm surface water, by the technique known as ocean
thermal energy conversion. Second, the cold water, being
much richer than the surface water in the nutrients needed
for support of life, would promote the production of abundant
food and other materials in a wet Green Machine. Plenty of
people already went to sea for fun—yachtsmen, sportfisher-
men, skin divers—and if some were willing to go into the hostile, alien environment of space, many more volunteers should
be available for new settlements in the far more congenial
setting of the Earth's oceans.

For those who regarded information as the product that
would count for most in the economies and ways of life of
the 1980s and beyond, a cornucopia of another kind was in
prospect: the Total Information Machine. With satellites and
fiber-optic cables offering essentially unlimited channels of
communication, right to the individual's home or office, there
seemed to be no limit except human powers of concentration
to the amount of information that could be shuttled around
within and between countries. Anyone might in principle have
quick access to all human knowledge in library-recorded forms,
to current news and scholarly research, to information services
of many kinds, and to entertainment on demand.

This was often summed up by saying that a person would
be able to sit at home, with a keyboard and visual display,
and do work, call up friends on a video telephone, read books,
watch movies, play games, and do the shopping, without ever
leaving the house. It was a weird idea, strongly reminiscent
of the Disembodied Brain and highly ambiguous in respect
of human relationships, with "electronic loneliness" looming
for many people riveted to their visual-display units.

The Total Information System might be centralizing or decentralizing in its effects, depending on issues of ownership and control. But it would be disruptive of social systems if human beings retracted into electronic shells, rejecting their local communities while networking with carbon-copy acquaintances in far-flung places. Systems engineers might be disappointed if people insisted on going out, traveling, and meeting other human beings in the usual serendipitous fashion. However it turned out in its applications and modes, the Total Information Machine fully matched the promise of material benefits from other conceivable systems.

The Santa Claus Machine eating rocks; the Green Machines living on sunlight, carbon dioxide, and water; Space Cities assembled from the surface dust of the moon and running on spare solar energy; and the Ocean Cities turning watery wastes into scenes of abundant life: when all these technological possibilities were put together, one promise of technology in the late twentieth century was the elimination of poverty. Technically, it was a straightforward task to make a paradise of the planet Earth in which no one need go hungry, be cold, or lack the resources necessary for an interesting and healthy life.

There was no longer any excuse whatever for letting children starve, or condemning so many of their parents to unrewarded drudgery. Technology made it ever easier for people to treat their fellow human beings with humanity and to advance from the economics of scarcity, greed, and jealousy to a social philosophy of shared abundance. If science and technology could only be used for humane and constructive purposes, their promise was brighter than ever before. Yet their main tendencies were in different and much darker directions, threatening the species with misery, loss of freedom, and death.

The Misery Machines

Forerunners of the Santa Claus Machine appeared in a sinister guise, in the real world of the late twentieth century, as destroyers of jobs. Overproduction was the bane of manufacturing industries as well as the farmers, and robotization made matters worse for individual workers. No great inventiveness was needed to imagine arrangements that would help the unemployed to feel more like ladies and gentlemen of leisure, than the outcasts of industrial society; or more rationally to share work and wages so that everyone had more leisure. But the vested interests resisting social change included the ordinary folk who had jobs and were earning good money.

To have so many people, including aggressive young males, rejected by their local, national, and global economies was a recipe for crime and social unrest. Increasing problems of "law and order" hastened the advent of new technologies for policing. Updating George Orwell's rather primitive technology of surveillance, the Big Brother Machine would use the resources of the Total Information Machine to achieve near-total vigilance on the activities of all citizens. For example, everyone might have to wear an electronic bracelet that signaled his or her whereabouts and conversations through the telephone network. Central "intelligent" computers would look for signs of illegal or unusual behavior.

Another potentially dangerous aspect of information technology in the late twentieth century was epitomized in the Smart Aleck Machine. An intense international competition to develop the fifth-generation computer hastened the quest for artificial intelligence and a machine that, in some important sense, would be smarter than the human brain. Some of the engineers and software experts involved spoke quite openly about designing the successor of the human species: superintelligences who would treat us like pets, and usurp our role as potential colonizers of the solar system and the galaxy. Those involved with the Japanese fifth-generation computer visualized it being used to solve social problems. Putting that in plainer language, machines would tell people how to run their lives.

The Smart Aleck Machine was expected to hit the professions first, as "expert systems" distilled the knowledge and methods of physicians, lawyers, engineers, and the like into software packages performing better than the average practitioner. To make a machine truly cleverer than a human being was difficult, because of the central importance of natural human language. Yet some people imagined that existing computers were smarter than they, and were ready to surrender to them many political, business, and military decisions. That meant granting power to the personnel who wrote the programs. Experts who knew how many errors were present in typical programs admitted to being terrified by the degree of trust already accorded to pseudo-intelligent computers in defense systems. False alarms that occurred in missile early-warning systems were not just mishaps—they were inevitable.

Worst of all the promises of science and technology was the Doomsday Machine. Invented as a theoretical concept by nuclear strategists exploring the limits of deterrence, the Doomsday Machine was a system that destroyed all human life—the person who set it off as well as his enemies, and all the neutrals too. Anyone who wanted to give it a literal meaning could imagine, for example, a number of large H-bombs carried in merchant ships and doped with material such as cobalt that was intended to cloak the world in intense and persistent radioactive fallout. By detonating such bombs at all latitudes, the perpetrator could make sure everyone had a fatal dose.

Although there was no sign of such a crazy system, there was a sufficient supply of crazy nation-states in the world to make the eventual appearance of a real Doomsday Machine quite likely. Meanwhile the nuclear arsenals of the world approximated a Doomsday Machine, at least for the inhabitants of the Northern Hemisphere. Highly accurate missiles entering service circa 1980 threatened the missiles and command systems of the other side and shifted nuclear strategy from a simple tit-for-tat to preoccupation with the first strike. The danger was not that one party or the other in the superpower confrontation would gratuitously start a nuclear war. But either side might be driven to push the button by paranoid logic. If A thought that B thought that A was about to attack, B must try to get his blow in first, and therefore A had better strike right away.

The biotechnological equivalent of the Doomsday Machine was the Doomsday Bug, at the terminus of inventions in biological weaponry. The clever techniques of microbiology and molecular medicine, which promised major new offensives against human diseases, were equally applicable to the creation of new diseases, or the preservation of old ones as weapons.

Apart from the manufacture of extremely potent toxins, such as those produced by *Fusarium* fungi, the main possibility in biological warfare would be to release a deadly virus or bacterium that would infect enemy troops and civilians, and propagate itself in the natural way. The aggressor nation would have stockpiles of vaccine ready for the protection of its own people. The disease-causing agent would be one to which the target population had no resistance: it might be a genetically engineered novelty, or a rare or exotic natural pathogen. The potential military importance of disease was demonstrated in Spanish conquests of the sixteenth century. The warlike Aztecs and Incas succumbed to unfamiliar smallpox and measles, enabling small bands of Spanish troops to take possession of a continent.

Smallpox was totally eradicated from the world in 1977, in medical science's finest hour, and the World Health Organization subsequently decided that only two laboratories in the world, in Atlanta and Moscow, should retain cultures of the smallpox virus. South Africa defied the ruling. In *The Gene Factory* (1985), the biotechnology writer John Elkington commented:

> With the elimination of smallpox in the wild and the falling immunity of the world's population to the disease, it is not difficult to imagine why South Africa might want to hold onto the cultures. The National Institute for Virology's director admitted that the decision "was not taken for scientific reasons."

Abundant arsenals of potential weapons existed in microbiological laboratories the world over. Genetic engineering could improve their military effectiveness by increasing the virulence of the bugs and ensuring their novelty to human immune systems. The weapons could also be targeted on categories of people distinguished by their genetics and biochemistry: for example, a disease that killed only men, only women, only the young, or only the old. AIDS offered a natural example of a disease tailored to a particular form of behavior: sexual promiscuity. An "ethnic bug" might be adapted to kill people of high or low levels of skin pigmentation.

Diseases of animals and plants offered another category of potential biological weapons for attacking an enemy's food supplies and cash crops. This could be done clandestinely over a period of years, perhaps to destabilize the regime. As people became more alert to such dangers, a new source of international tension and war became apparent. Naturally occurring diseases of plants, animals, or humans might be blamed on a hostile neighbor. The suspicions might be matters of fantasy, but the allegations were not. The Chinese accused the Americans of releasing germ-laden flies during the Korean War, the Cubans blamed the Americans for an outbreak of swine fever, and the Americans alleged that the Russians supplied the "yellow rain" fungal toxins that appeared in Laos and Cambodia.

Biological weapons were also called the poor man's H-bomb. To say so overstated the difficulties of making nuclear weapons, but the facilities needed for biological weapons were more widely available and easier to conceal. Any well-equipped hospital path lab, vaccine plant, or brewery could be adapted to military purposes. The protection of one's own population remained a more elaborate and more public task. And as the released diseases might mutate and return to plague the inventor, all deadly biological weapons had a doomsday quality.

The misery machines in this second group of technological extremes were closer to feasibility and more likely to be realized than most of the fine promises for a better life embodied in the earlier group. In a malign feedback, unemployment, Big-Brother surveillance, usurpation by computer, and the risk of nuclear war all interacted in a dangerous way. More and more nations were acquiring a nuclear-weapon capability. As military systems became ever more falsely sophisticated, people in many walks of life began to think it was no longer a question of whether there would be a nuclear war, but when.

Twilight at Noon

The actuarially minded could look back and conservatively assess the chance of a major nuclear war between the superpowers during the period from 1945 to 1985 at 50 percent. A single event, the Cuban missile crisis of 1962, could account for 40 percent; President Kennedy, who led the American team in that confrontation, is said to have rated the probability between one-third and one-half. The remaining 10 percent risk was a modest figure to assign to all the other ways nuclear war might have started, especially in view of the false alarms known to have put nuclear forces on full alert, which was very frightening for the other side. Taking account of the calculus of fear surrounding missiles of high accuracy, made worse by anti-satellite systems on both sides, the next interval corresponding to a 50 percent risk of nuclear war would be shorter —perhaps twenty-five years. If so, nuclear war would be more likely than not during the thirty years from 1986 to 2115. The same level of risk persisting indefinitely would give nuclear war a probability of 87 percent during the lifetime of a child born in 1985, who might otherwise live for seventy-five years.

In 1982, an atmospheric scientist working in Mainz, Paul Crutzen, joined with John Birks, an American environmental scientist, to write a report for the Royal Swedish Academy of Sciences on the effects of nuclear war on the Earth's atmosphere. The report appeared in the Swedish journal *Ambio* under the title "Twilight at Noon," and it sketched the effects on the world's climate of the smoke that would be released into the atmosphere from forest fires ignited during a nuclear war. It gave the human species its first news of the nuclear winter that menaced it. Within months, Richard Turco and others at Cornell University were pointing out that the smoke from burning cities would have worse effects than that from the forest fires.

Until then, everyone agreed that the consequences of nuclear war would be indescribably dreadful in the war zones, but scientific assessments of the long-term, global effects were reassuring. Cancers and malformed babies would appear as a result of radioactive fallout, but these would add at most only a few percent to the cases occurring for more natural reasons. There were worries about the destruction of much of the Earth's ozone layer, which gave protection against the ultra-violet rays from the sun. On the whole, though, it seemed that disruptions of trade would be a worse problem for people living far from the war zones, than any changes in the physical conditions of life. Nobody had stopped to think about the smoke, or how it would obscure the sun and chill the world.

The prestigious International Council of Scientific Unions mobilized 300 scientists from thirty countries to investigate the nuclear winter, through its Scientific Committee on Problems of the Environment, SCOPE. Reporting in 1985, they confirmed the dire effects to be expected when nuclear explosions ignited fires in the wood, paper, plastics, asphalt, and fossil-fuel stores of cities, and released many millions of tons of black carbon soot into the Earth's atmosphere. Soot would have the opposite effect to a greenhouse; it would let the Earth's heat escape into space while blocking the light and heat from the sun. Computer models explored the likely development and spread of the pall of smoke around the world. Although it avoided the term "nuclear winter," the SCOPE report depicted a darkened and chilled planet where billions of people in nonbelligerent countries would face death by starvation.

In the middle latitudes of the Northern Hemisphere, where most of the explosions would occur, the intensity of the sun's rays would drop to just a few percent of normal daylight. This would go down to less than 1 percent under the densest patches of smoke, where temperatures on the ground could plummet to 20° or 40° C below the normal in a matter of days. After a war fought during the summer, average temperatures in the middle latitudes of the Northern Hemisphere would be down to those normally experienced in the fall or early winter, for a period of weeks or more, and outbreaks of frosty air could afflict wide areas. The smoke could also place a lid on the lower atmosphere, suppressing the vertical circulation responsible

for rain and snow, and perhaps eliminating for a period the
monsoon rains on which farmers in the subtropics depended.
The pall might last for more than a year and cause persistent
cooling.

Combustible materials were so concentrated in large industrial cities that even a "small" nuclear war which burned out
only a hundred of them would generate 50–150 million tons
of smoke; 30 million tons of carbon soot remaining in the atmosphere would be sufficient to cause very severe cooling. In
this perspective, any talk of reducing nuclear arsenals by, say,
half was meaningless; the remaining missiles could still cause
a nuclear winter several times over.

The SCOPE experts studying the effects of the nuclear winter on agriculture itemized many factors that could disrupt
food production, but these revolved around the question of
whether crop plants would have enough warmth, light, and
rainfall to mature before chills or frosts killed them. The consensus of the team was that the cooling effect alone, for nuclear
war occurring between spring and early autumn, would be
sufficient to wipe out virtually all crops in the middle latitudes
of the Northern Hemisphere. In the tropics, many crop plants
would succumb even to a brief chilling. Rice production would
be eliminated in the Northern Hemisphere, and perhaps even
in the Southern Hemisphere, where the smoke veil would be
much thinner.

Beyond the climatic effects, the disruptions of human activity
and trade by nuclear war would hit food production. The inputs
into agriculture that had helped to increase world food production dramatically could be lost, including fertilizer, pesticides,
fuel for water pumps and tractors, and vaccines against deadly
diseases of animals. Many of the world's long-term reserves
of food lay in countries that would be likely targets for nuclear
attacks.

While a moderate-sized nuclear war might kill up to a billion
people in the targeted countries by direct effects of the nuclear
explosions, calculations in the SCOPE report indicated that a
further two to four billion would die of starvation if the nuclear
winter halted food production over large areas of the Earth.
Great uncertainties surrounded the numbers, but it was easier

to make them come out worse rather than better. For example, the entire population of India, more than 700 million people, could perish. The SCOPE authors were certain that the Earth's human population was much more vulnerable to indirect effects of nuclear war on food production than to the direct effects of the war itself. In the report's dry language: "Risk is therefore exported from combatant to noncombatant countries."

This was the culminating scandal of the nuclear confrontation. In a nuclear war between the Soviet Union and the United States, for every Russian and American killed outright, several men, women, and children in distant places such as Nigeria or the Philippines would be condemned to die of starvation. Yet the superpowers maintained thousands of missiles armed with nuclear warheads in combat readiness, available for launching at a few minutes' notice, and capable of stealing the sunshine from the world's farms.

The delicate efforts of the plant biotechnologists, coaxing the chloroplasts to convert as much as possible of the sun's radiant energy to plant growth, were pitiful compared with the huge drive in military technology directed toward switching off the sun. Even the U.S. Star Wars program, intended to destroy missiles in space, seemed likely to protect missile silos rather than cities, thereby preserving the warheads for stoking the fires on the other side of the North Pole. The leaders Gorbachev and Reagan, beaming at each other at a summit conference while failing to agree about anything of consequence, were latter-day Midases whose touch could turn everything to soot.

The reactions of people habituated to the nuclear arms race and its rhetoric were complacent. In an editorial on the SCOPE report, the *New York Times* (September 29th, 1985) commented:

> The main message is that deterrence must not be allowed to fail, and long before any meaningful defense can be achieved, the arsenals held for retaliation need to be reduced to the smallest possible size.

The newspaper evidently visualized business as usual for the nuclear warriors and their deterrents, and for the endless dance of the arms-control negotiators. The superpowers would go on treating the planet as their plaything. Their behavior was undermining even the modest achievements of the diplomats, in the Nonproliferation and Antiballistic Missile Treaties.

Sooner or later a criminally insane leader of one nation or another would make a real Doomsday Machine, perhaps updated as a generator of smoke rather than radioactivity. Adolf Hitler and Idi Amin were just two of the dangerous people who achieved significant power in the modern world. In his book *Crazy States* (1971) the Israeli strategic analyst Yehezkel Dror noted an opinion of some experts that a radioactive doomsday system would require significant but not tremendous resources. Dror went on:

> These experts think that it is only the taboo on the nature of the idea and its obvious uselessness which inhibit work in that direction. . . . a counterstylistic crazy state will not be bound by the taboos surrounding a doomsday machine. For a crazy martyr state, a doomsday machine may be an obviously preferable instrument.

Hope ceased to be a virtue when it tolerated the intolerable and trusted untrustworthy leaders to make matters better. Forty years after Hiroshima was time enough for reasonable people to shed all hope that the world's nuclear weapons might be negotiated away, or even reduced to such low levels that their detonation would not cause nuclear winter. Marches and demonstrations publicized the problem and eased the consciences of those taking part, but they failed to change the nuclear-weapons policies of nation-states.

Quiet despair, tinged with regret for the much better world that might have been, was an inept response for the most adaptable animals on Earth. The human species had to discover how to cope with "exported risk" and give its children a chance of living. The biologically appropriate reaction to mortal danger, when brought about by actions of one's own species, was well-directed anger. But against whom?

Should Science Be Stopped?

The physicist Richard Feynman, driving Freeman Dyson from
Cornell to New Mexico in 1948, measured in his mind's eye
the distances from ground zero as they passed through each
city, and wondered how people could go on living in places
like New York after the destruction of Hiroshima. Yet for forty
years intelligent men and women went about their business
in the nuclear-armed states as if nothing had changed. Adults
encouraged moral attitudes in their children, including the
love of animals and Presidents, that bore little relation to the
stark evils they were likely to face during their lives.

"When a man knows he is to be hanged in a fortnight,"
Samuel Johnson supposed, "it concentrates his mind wonder-
fully." The prospect of mass extermination was less productive
of clear thinking. Far less intellectual effort went into averting
nuclear war than designing new weaponry. Surgeons trans-
planted hearts to save the lives of individuals and paused to
observe that they could not cope with millions of casualties
in a nuclear war. Scientists continued with their researches
to enlarge human knowledge, even though they knew the military establishments monitored all their discoveries for anything
that might harm an cncmy.

Nevertheless, some scientists were close to despair. One was
the British physicist Martin Ryle, who helped to develop radar
during World War II and then became a founding father of
radio astronomy. He invented the aperture-synthesis method,
whereby distant galaxies could be examined in detail by a set
of small radio dishes moved around to simulate, or "synthesize,"
a much larger dish. For this work he won the Nobel Prize
for Physics in 1974. Thereafter he devoted much of his time
to campaigning against nuclear weapons and in favor of windmills.

In 1983, Ryle wrote an anguished letter to the Brazilian scientist Carlos Chagas. It came to light after Ryle's death in 1984.
In it he declared:

> At the end of World War II I decided that never again would I
> use my scientific knowledge for military purposes; astronomy

seemed about as far removed as possible. But in succeeding years we developed new techniques for making very powerful radio telescopes; these techniques have been perverted for improving radar and sonar systems. A sadly large proportion of the PhD students we have trained have taken the skills they have learnt in these and other areas into the field of defence. I am left at the end of my scientific life with the feeling that it would have been better to have become a farmer in 1946. One can, of course, argue that somebody else would have done it anyway, and so we must face the most fundamental of questions.

Should fundamental science (in some areas now, others will emerge later) be stopped? [Ryle's emphasis.]

A superficial or supercilious answer would be that stopping science was impossible because it was built into the workings of the modern industrial nation-states. Communist regimes claimed to be based on science; capitalist regimes cherished the freedom of the individual to inquire and to innovate. Education was a huge industry underpinning other industries, and research was always needed to stop teachers telling too many lies about Nature.

Yet Ryle's question echoed ancient myths of Prometheus and Faust; also Winston Churchill's remark that "The next stone age may come on the silver wings of science." Was it not immoral relentlessly to pursue new knowledge, wherever it might lead, whatever its consequences? In a half-answer of his own Ryle commented: "We do not *have* to understand the evolution of galaxies." Coming from an eminent astronomer this was like a poet offering to surrender his pen.

The inhabitants of Europe and North America, the citadels of scientific research, traced their traditions to the city-states of ancient Greece. The Greeks gambled on a belief that most human beings were kindly and reasonable. From that proposition others flowed. Individuals were important, and they should have great freedom to run their own lives and to play their democratic part in running their communities.

Knowledge was good. That was another consequence of the belief that human beings were on the whole kindly and reasonable. There was nothing that a rational being should not know, even though there might be many things they should not do with the knowledge. The information that hemlock was poisonous need not be an inducement to murder; discovering the fission of heavy atoms entailed no obligation to make bombs.

Science marched ahead with the consent of the people. Reincarnated in modern form in seventeenth-century Europe, the Greek tradition became extremely strong, thanks to mutual support between the strands of individualism, democracy, and the pursuit of knowledge. And science paid off magnificently, both in understanding the natural world and in making useful inventions. Although the population explosion was regrettable, it was a mark of fantastic material success. By that biological test, knowledge was plainly a good thing—unless, of course, a population crash was pending, in which case the large numbers only multiplied the eventual misery.

The link between the twin beliefs in the virtues of knowledge and the virtues of people remained indissoluble. If human beings were unkind and unreasonable, then they could not be trusted with dangerous information, and knowledge was a bad thing. Molecular biologists who complained that warnings about the military possibilities of genetic engineering were putting ideas into people's heads overlooked the unwritten pact of mutual trust between scientists and other people.

Censorship and secrecy were symptoms of mistrust. The medieval church placed Galileo under house arrest, and Stalin's regime sent geneticists to prison camps, because of fears that the evidence of science might distract people from higher truths about the perfection of the heavens or the perfectibility of man. A counter example of high trust in human nature was the Freedom of Information Act in the U.S., one consequence of which was that anyone could get hold of official documents explaining how to make a nuclear bomb.

By the mid-1980s, the latest hopes of checking the arms race were foundering on disagreements between the superpowers about strategic defenses in space, and it seemed that after 2500 years the Greek gamble had failed. The bold theories and delicate experiments that over the centuries laid bare nature's secrets brought the human species at last to the autumn before nuclear winter. Whether the odds against nuclear war might run out in a hundred minutes or a hundred years, to expect any other outcome was no longer reasonable. By the test of doing more harm than good, science already appeared to be illegitimate, and the cynical answer to Ryle's question was that the bombs themselves would put the brakes on fundamental research.

Moral pangs among the scientists were a triviality compared with the physical torments by fire and frost that their inventions promised to let loose on billions of people. Yet any real hope of escaping the catastrophe would depend on understanding exactly what had gone wrong in the compact between scientists and other people. The problem was a failure of wisdom, as distinct from knowledge. The London philosopher Nicholas Maxwell quoted Socrates as the founder and great practitioner of the philosophy of wisdom:

> Esteemed friend, citizen of Athens, the greatest city in the world, so outstanding in both intelligence and power, aren't you ashamed to care so much to make all the money you can, and to advance your reputation and prestige—while for truth and wisdom and the improvement of your soul you have no care or worry?

In his book *From Knowledge to Wisdom* (1984), Maxwell blamed the irrationality and inhumanity of the world on the successors of Socrates who, right down to modern times, thought that they should scrupulously restrict themselves in their professional capacity to the pursuit of knowledge. By doing so, scientists, scholars, and teachers ignored what Maxwell called their "most vital professional task: to help promote the cooperative rational search for what is of most value in personal and social life."

In Maxwell's diagnosis, scientists suffered from a "rationalistic neurosis," in which they repeatedly misrepresented their aims. They claimed to be bent on discovering factual truth and deliberately ignoring all questions of value; in fact, they were aiming to discover factual truth of value to scientists, and of value to those who paid for their research. The more energetically scientists pursued the fiction of value-free research, the harder it was for them to achieve the ideal aim of discovering factual truth of value for creating a more just and wiser world.

Maxwell's analysis was fair, although he seemed too ready to throw the baby of attempted objectivity out with the bathwater of selfishness. It was also doubtful that even a concerted effort by scientists, scholars, and teachers to rediscover wisdom in the Socratic tradition could arrive at a consensus, never mind changing the world rapidly enough to avert catastrophe. The behavior of scholars and scientists was in any case molded and limited by the social systems to which they belonged.

Socrates drank his hemlock because he was convicted by a democratic court of corrupting the young. One allegation was that he was the teacher of Alcibiades, a commander whose recklessness hastened the fall of the Athenian empire. Was a teacher then responsible for his student's actions? Any suggestion that the world could be radically improved by wiser teaching seemed to assume that the answer was yes. So, for that matter, did the idea of stopping science—as if the deletion of items like nuclear fission or genetic engineering from the syllabuses would somehow be a cure for wickedness.

The moral and philosophical crisis about science was real and urgent at the end of the twentieth century. But internal failings and "neuroses" in science, serious though they were, could not be blamed for the division of the world into armed camps, or the disgraceful contrast between riches and starvation. Science and technology created few new moral issues. More often they dramatized and exacerbated aspects of immoral behavior much older than organized science. In this, science was more victim than criminal.

The Greeks were not wrong in thinking knowledge a good thing; nor were people on the whole unfit to be trusted with potent information. But their nation-states were palpably unfit, and they were the biggest spenders on science and technology. In the 1980s, defense research budgets were soaring, and at least a quarter of the world's scientists and engineers were occupied with military developments. Those working in the weapons laboratories regarded themselves sincerely as patriotic citizens, only doing their duty as perceived by the legal governments of their countries. Would it not be intolerable if scientists presumed to dictate policy?

In the three-cornered system of the public, the government,

and science, something had to give. Dr. Strangelove's solution, in Stanley Kubrick's 1960s movie, was to be rid of the public, with officials and scientists surviving the nuclear war in their deep shelters. The arrangements of the 1980s for trying to preserve vestiges of national government from nuclear attack foreshadowed just such an outcome, as if the culminating aim of civilization was to ensure that the last man alive would be a bureaucrat with a geiger counter.

Martin Ryle's tentative proposal to eliminate science evidently envisaged that government and people would have a breathing space in which to solve the problems created by existing technology. But if it came to a showdown, scientists could make some powerful claims for their activities. In the first place, the human world was still full of erroneous theories and false information that were frustrating efforts to create a healthier planet, and science still had plenty to do in clearing them away. A practical consideration was that new technology would be needed to feed and employ a doubled world population without desecrating the planet.

The most telling point in science's favor was that it belonged to the public as a right. Irrespective of social systems, and as a fact of biology, human beings were inquisitive about their place in the universe and the properties of the living and inanimate furniture of their planet. To stop science, it would be necessary to cut out the tongues of the children, who persisted in asking about fundamental matters that adults preferred to gloss over: "Why is the sun hot?" for example. After a thousand generations the question was answered by science, which could be regarded as a system for sustaining childlike curiosity in adulthood. In this case, the explanation of the sun's power led directly and swiftly to the H-bomb.

The third and only acceptable way to cure the fateful triangle of the public, government, and science was to change the government. Replacing one set of rulers by another was not enough, because nation-states of widely differing cultures and political creeds had shown themselves ready to develop nuclear weapons. The organization of the world was breaking under the strain of scientific discovery, and the nation-states themselves had to go.

Scientists could recover legitimacy for their craft by helping to dissolve the nation-states. The special relevance of the green machines was that they offered an exceptional opportunity— perhaps the very last chance—for scientists to show they were on the side of the human species, against its warmongering institutions. If they wanted to continue their researches and still be able to look their children in the eye, scientists would have to be ready to join with others in committing a kind of treason.

The Rise and Fall of the Nation-State

Hints of wisdom of the kind that commentators like Nicholas Maxwell craved came from a neglected source: archeology. While mainstream science was employing radioactive elements for quite different purposes, archeologists in their small groups found that radiocarbon could clarify the timescale of human prehistory. Scientific archeology also used large-scale surveys and statistical methods to help transform their knowledge of the past. Where their predecessors had concentrated on great monuments, the new prehistorians examined the lives of ordinary people in their ecological setting. And their discoveries tore to shreds certain dangerous myths about human nature and the origin of warfare.

A standard view, right across the political spectrum, was that for all its faults modern civilization was a distinct improvement on the entirely brutish lives of primitive ancestors. Against this view could be set Jean-Jacques Rousseau's image of the noble savage, but that creature was seen sentimentally rather than as any serious model for the modern world. To many it seemed self-evident that social systems evolved onward and upward, in much the same way as life itself had developed progressively from bacteria to intelligent primates. For Marxists, the supposed discovery of the laws of social history pointed the way forward to the ideal communist state. By the 1980s the idea of reliable progress in the course of natural evolution looked increasingly dubious; more emphatically, the findings of the archeologists put paid to simpleminded confidence about social progress.

Among the discoveries about prehistory that were particularly telling, one set concerned the lively intelligence of the hunter-gatherers of the late Paleolithic era. Modern human beings like ourselves appeared about 40,000 years ago, and by ingenuity and adaptability they were able quite quickly to occupy all the habitable continents of the world. They prospered at all latitudes from the polar ice to the equator. Their technical competence was manifest in tools, hunting weapons, and ornaments made with unprecedented skill. The paintings of animals in the Lascaux caves in France, 17,000 years old, showed sensitivity and flair equal to anything of modern times.

A second set of findings with special relevance to the modern world concerned prehistoric biotechnology. The multiple Neolithic revolutions that initiated agriculture were amazing not only in their identification and improvement by breeding of all the best crops and farm animals, but also in adapting them to different ecological settings in efficient green systems. Woolly sheep and the milking cows were essentially human inventions; so, more obviously, were woven textiles, brewing and wine making, and the manufacture of butter and cheese. The advent of the plow and the wheel between 4000 and 3500 B.C. had far-reaching effects on agriculture and society. Another kind of sophistication was evident in clay tokens of various shapes. Accountants in the Near East used these symbols before they invented writing on clay tablets.

A well-studied early farming culture was that of the Bandkeramik people who grew wheat and barley on the rich loess soils of Central and Western Europe. They flourished between 5800 and 4900 B.C. by the raw radiocarbon dates, or about a thousand years earlier when the dates were adjusted, and systematic excavations, especially in Germany and the Netherlands, revealed salient facts about them. Their houses and graves were all similar, showing that their society was egalitarian. It was also efficient. Although these were Europe's very first farmers, they achieved productivities high enough to support a population density more than half as great as that attained in medieval Germany some 7000 years later. And during nearly a thousand years of the Bandkeramik culture there was no sign of organized warfare. Only at the end did military earthworks appear, when the people tried to defend themselves against unidentified invaders.

For a world on the brink of nuclear catastrophe, the most significant archeological findings were those that traced the origins of modern social institutions. In place of the old idea of steady evolution there emerged a richer picture of social systems evolving and decaying, and new systems arising at their geographical peripheries. Many features of the modern world could be traced to a relatively quick succession of events in Mesopotamia and Egypt between 3600 and 3100 B.C. These culminated in the invention of systematic warfare, in the confidence trick that created the first states.

The earliest known tax demands, from Uruk in southern Mesopotamia in about 3600 B.C., took the form of clay tokens wrapped in a clay envelope; later envelopes were embellished with pictures of bound prisoners. At Gawra in northern Mesopotamia, around the same time, signs of blatant class distinctions appeared in a minority of rich burials. Some 300 years later, from the Nile Valley of Egypt, came the first signs of warfare occurring as a way of life instead of an occasional calamity. These coincided with the rise of warrior kings, followed within a century or two by the creation of the first authoritarian states, in Egypt and Mesopotamia.

The long hindsight of archeology put all states and all warfare in a startling new perspective. So far from states taming unruly and violent people, and teaching them to live in peace, the truth was exactly the opposite. Warriors of the new states actively cultivated warfare as the means of keeping their own subjects under control. Philosophers and behavioral scientists who tried for centuries to blame endless war making on the bestiality in human nature had missed the point entirely.

Chronic warfare was a social institution, invented at a specifiable date for the purpose of creating a new kind of social system that allowed some people to lord it over others. It was a protection racket: pay your taxes, obey my orders, and I shall defend you against those terrible people down the river. The other warrior king down the river was saying the same thing, in a symbiosis of terror. It would be pleasant if one could record that warlike states were an aberration confined to the Old World, but the Amerindians of Middle America reinvented them around 1250 B.C.

For the system to work, actual wars were necessary from time to time, lest the fear of war should abate and the authority of the state grow weaker. The frequency of major wars, typically once in a generation, became understandable in this perspective. Pretexts were easy to find. Imperial conquests were special sweeteners for the soldiers and citizens, while religious and political ideologies served to stir real passions.

Permanent armies made repression of the population very easy. Nevertheless, alternative forms of state government evolved. In Greece, the navy was often more important than the army, with war galleys rowed by volunteers serving as the chief weapons. Sailors were less suited to crowd control than soldiers, and the military bias, as well as dispersal to isolated cities and islands, may have encouraged the brief flowering of democracy in Greece. This mode of government allowed more frequent changes in the faces of the rulers, but the basic compact did not change. The demagogue said, "Pay your taxes, obey my orders, and I shall defend you against those terrible people across the water."

By medieval times states had evolved into feudal regimes and city-states ruled by petty lords or plutocrats, and their characteristic weapons were castles and knights in armor. The advent of gunpower made them obsolescent, because castles and city walls could be literally undermined, and also because armaments were becoming very expensive. The contest for maritime empires, waged with gun-carrying sailing ships, accelerated the development of the modern nation-state, which centralized political power and mobilized the skills of large countries in the cause of a new religion: nationalism. Modern science prospered as a servant of the nation-states, although it liked to assert the international nature of knowledge.

The Netherlands, France, and England were pioneers of the modern nation-state; revolts in American colonies created a string of new nation-states. Italy, Germany, and Japan were comparative latecomers to the "comity of nations." Although there were plenty of differences among their constitutions, ranging from absolute monarchies or dictatorships to genuine democracies, their similarities were at least as striking, especially that the first call on taxes was for defense. Scientists and engineers invented new weapons at a high rate, and from the mid nineteenth century onward the technological arms race became continuous. A succession of ferocious wars introduced high explosives, machine guns, submarines, aircraft, battle tanks, guided missiles, and nuclear weapons.

By the twentieth century the nation-state had become the norm of government, and the collapse of the European empires in Asia and Africa after 1945 brought a host of new nation-states into existence. Sometimes their frontiers, inherited from colonial administrations, bore little relationship to ethnic boundaries. For example the Ashanti people of West Africa were split between the French-speaking Togo and Ivory Coast, with English-speaking Ashanti sandwiched between them in Ghana. But all of the new nation-states had their flags and national anthems, their football teams, their commanders-in-chief, and their enemies of the moment. As Arnold Toynbee remarked:

> This present world-wide cult of national sovereignty is strange, considering that the concept originated in one part only of the human race—the Western part—and that, even there, did not become prevalent until a fairly recent stage of Western history.

The governments of the nation-states found plenty of ways besides warfare to busy themselves. They supervised education, industry, and agriculture, and took responsibility for managing the economy. Governments ran schemes for caring for the sick, the poor, and the aged. Aid to poor countries was added to the list, as people looked to central government for leadership and financial help in more and more areas of activity. But even good-natured welfare states remained in principle warfare states. In the national leaders' club, the military dictators outnumbered any other group of members.

The game of statehood continued as it had done for 5000

years. In the world's most powerful nation-state, Republicans and Democrats outbid one another in their promises of firm resistance to the external enemy. Their Soviet opponents used the American threat to bolster a repressive regime. Among the players of the game—politicians, generals, bureaucrats, defense scientists—each side needed the other. Arms control might be tolerable, but far-reaching disarmament, never. Amid untidy geopolitical, revolutionary, and religious quarrels, which killed 20 million people in some 150 wars between 1945 and 1985, at least one had the classic qualities of a demonstration fight of warrior kings: the Falklands war between Britain and Argentina in 1982.

After one short century of a world of nation-states, the game was almost played out. Nuclear weapons broke the ancient compact of the state. No quantity of taxes, no granting of authority to national leaders, could defend civilian populations against a downpour of missile warheads carrying H-bombs. Some awareness of this broken promise may have inspired President Reagan to set such store by the Strategic Defense Initiative. If so, he had less feeling for the hardware difficulties and software impossibilities of the Star Wars concept, than for the growing anxieties of his citizens.

Just as gunpowder made feudal regimes obsolete, so nuclear explosives spelt doom for the social system of the modern world. The power of the weapons was peculiarly well suited to taking out cities and smashing the political and economic structures of a nation-state, along with a large fraction of the population. Whatever else might survive a major nuclear attack, it would not be the political constitution. Indeed, the constitutions of parliamentary democracies were already compromised, because high-speed missiles removed from the lawmakers any control over declarations of war, if it came to a nuclear exchange.

In the long retrospective described here, the very existence of nation-states turned out to be the principal cause of danger in the world. They functioned effectively in the era of gunpowder, and disastrously but survivably during world wars fought with high explosives. One way or another they would soon cease to exist, like the god-kings of Egypt and the iron-suited barons of medieval Europe. Either the system of nation-states would self-destruct in a nuclear war, or the citizens would, in the nick of time, understand why they were in such danger, and dismember their nation-states.

The Empire and the Village

The organization of the world could change toward entities larger than nation-states, or smaller. The Soviet empire, the North Atlantic Treaty Organization, and the European Economic Community were examples of regional groupings, but they did not seem likely to eliminate the risk of nuclear war. Under the Treaty of Tlatelolco (1967) twenty-two nation-states of Latin America promised to prohibit all manufacture or possession of nuclear weapons in their continent. Suspicions persisted that the Brazilians and Argentinians were acquiring the capacity to make the bomb.

Anything intermediate in scale between nation-states and the whole planet might create a world like that described by George Orwell, in which three blocs permuted their alliances in unending conflict—acting, in effect, like big nation-states. The chief large-scale alternative was therefore a unitary world empire of all mankind. Conquest or assimilation of the entire planet by one nation or bloc might be one of the surest ways of preventing nuclear war for a long time to come. It would be difficult to accomplish without first having a nuclear war.

Other routes to a world empire looked possible in the late twentieth century. One was the *Pax Americana-Sovietica*, in which the two superpowers would combine to take charge of the world. Their primary purpose would be to eliminate all nuclear weapons except those in their own hands, and to suppress any development of new nuclear weapons. A glimpse of such a system in action occurred in 1977, when the U.S. and U.S.S.R. collaborated in using their spy satellites to monitor suspected preparations for a nuclear-weapons test in South Africa.

To Americans and Russians such a union might seem a wonderful resolution of their difficulties. They could shed their mutual suspicions in working together to keep the world safe from nuclear war. They could also seek to enforce the reduction of conventional armies, and police all disputes. More positively they could offer their combined expertise to solve outstanding economic and ecological problems, and so lead the rest of the world to prosperity. Other "great powers" could be represented in the directorate. Something quite like that was built into the UN Security Council, where five "great powers" were permanent members with power of veto; they had, though, no strong means of enforcing a collective decision.

The most that could be said in favor of U.S.-Soviet overlordship was that it might be preferable to nuclear war. To the rest of the world it would seem a lunatic solution. Having the two powers most responsible for creating the danger offering to cure the danger would be like seeing Mafia bosses take charge of the narcotics squad. To the Japanese and Chinese, it would seem as if the have-beens of the capitalist and communist realms were using their possession of the most nuclear weapons to try to prolong their reigns. In the Third World, the U.S.-Soviet directorate would appear as a new version of racist colonialism, enshrining the notion that only whites were fit to possess nuclear weapons and to tell everyone else how to live.

With plenty of people in the world detesting both the American and the Russian regimes, some would regard it as their patriotic, religious, or political duty to develop nuclear or biological weapons to challenge the authority of the directorate. Preventing this would require intense surveillance by a global Big Brother Machine. So this form of world empire would quickly degenerate into a planet-wide police state.

Commerce offered a faintly plausible route to world empire. A vigorous nation-state (Japan was an obvious candidate) or a multinational corporation might play a global game of Monopoly and win comprehensively. It would in effect buy up the world's key resources, and be in a position to tell the superpowers and everyone else how to behave: "Get rid of your bombs or we'll put your whole country out of work." Threatened nations might be strongly tempted to wipe all the banking score-boards clean with the nuclear electromagnetic pulse or electronic subterfuge. If that did not happen, and the economic victor prevailed, clandestine military reactions from the losers would again force the creation of a global police state.

A madman with a Doomsday Machine would be in the strongest position to become Emperor of the World. Given an irrational weapon, the crazier its owner acted the better, from the point of view of persuading the rest of the human species that he meant business. Once he had incinerated a city or two to demonstrate his contempt for human life, he could order the President of the United States to recite the Koran while standing on his head in the nude.

As there was no political, military, medical, or any other solution to the riddle of how to disobey someone able and willing to destroy all human life, the world would be self-policing. Everyone would strive to repress any behavior that might conceivably offend the emperor. A Doomsday dynasty could last a thousand years, or at least until one of the line absentmindedly pushed his button. It would be nice to suppose that neither the Russians nor the Americans would ever decide to "go crazy" and make a Doomsday Machine, but the temptations of power might prove too hard to resist, even for supposedly rational people.

This was not science fiction, and some experts took the possibility of a Doomsday Machine seriously enough to think that the organization of the world would have to change drastically to prevent the situation ever arising. As the Israeli strategic analyst Yehezkel Dror remarked:

> History is not made by highly probable behavior; rather, unusual and exceptional phenomena play critical roles in the shaping of human history.

In contrast with the mad emperor, the most orderly way to achieve a truly global social system would be for all nations to surrender their sovereignty to the United Nations or another invented body. They did so in many technical matters such as the allocation of radio frequencies or the standardization of vaccines. UN peacekeeping and technical assistance programs helped the world in various ways. But after forty years of existence the UN seemed further than ever from the sinking of political differences that would be required to create a world government. Even if by some miracle it happened, the practical problem of preventing the clandestine manufacture of nuclear weapons would once again float up to the top of the agenda, and even the voluntary world government would tend toward a police state.

The other method of replacing the nation-states was to dismantle them from the inside. The well-known separatist movements, including those of Quebec, Wales, Corsica, and the Basques and Catalans of Spain, did not offer an appropriate answer to the problem of the obsolete nation-states. The separatists often called themselves nationalists. Their aim, so far from eliminating nation-states, was to create new ones—small and inoffensive countries perhaps, but nevertheless able to fly their flags alongside those of Germany, Mexico, and the rest. If they ever achieved more than a modest increase in regional autonomy, they would want their own armed forces and commanders-in-chief.

Switzerland offered the best model for a thoroughly decentralized world. It possessed a powerful army, but no commander-in-chief. Switzerland was not a nation-state but a voluntary confederation of almost 3000 self-governing communes, each with an average population of about 2000 people. The communes grudgingly allowed the regional cantons and the federal council sufficient powers to enable the Swiss people to function effectively in the modern world, but theirs remained constitutionally a land of villages.

The ability of the Swiss to stay neutral and free from invasion, demonstrated in Europe's two major wars of the twentieth century, showed that a village-based organization was feasible and durable. The Swiss people also enjoyed a standard of living higher than that of the United States. In contrast with unproven and unconvincing dreams of a benign world government, the Swiss system was real, hard-bitten, and fully functional.

A world of a million villages could be a much safer place than a world of 170 nation-states. A system of armed neutrality, or determined self-defense, as practiced by the Swiss, could eliminate many of the risks of conventional warfare. On the other side of the world, villagers of Vietnam fought the world's most powerful nation and won.

In respect of nuclear warfare, too, the world of villages would be safer. Theodore Taylor, a former nuclear-weapons scientist, observed that villages were hardly worth attacking. A determined aggressor might divide and redivide his warheads to attack hundreds of small targets, but what would he gain from it? On the other hand, there would be no way of stopping truly autonomous villages or alliances of villages from developing their own nuclear weapons, so in this respect the system would not be as safe as a world police state. Yet it was hard to imagine how a village would use nuclear weapons except in self-defense. A Doomsday Machine remained a threat for villages, as for any other form of political organization. Chemical and biological weapons might be used for attacking the scattered populations. But if the worst happened, as the Vietnam War again illustrated, you could devastate a lot of villages without destroying a land and its people.

Critics predicted that the breakup of nation-states would create a scene like medieval Europe, where warfare between city-states and feudal domains was even more persistent than in later centuries. But although conflicts within a world of villages could not be ruled out, its main attraction was the lessening of the risk of total catastrophe. And beside the compelling military and political motives for wanting it, strong social reasons favored thorough-going decentralization.

Small Is Fashionable

If celibacy were not such a nuisance, Thomas More would have liked to be a monk. For the author of *Utopia* (1516) the monasteries of Europe were the model of a better life. Skeptical historians of utopian thought, Frank Manuel and Fritzie Manuel noted how often the Western ideas for a new society traced back to the ideals of Saint Benedict, who early in the sixth century founded the hilltop monastery of Monte Cassino between Naples and Rome.

In their small, isolated, self-governing, and self-sufficient realms, medieval monks found sustenance for their bodies and their souls. They escaped from the unbearable disorder of the world at large and sought a simple and frugal man-made order that gave them security and tranquility. A yearning for the same sort of life kept cropping up in nonreligious utopian schemes. It appeared, for example, in Francis Bacon's scientific House of Salomon; also in the "phalanxes" of Charles Fourier.

Writing in the early nineteenth century Fourier visualized human society reorganizing itself into cooperative agricultural settlements run on a profit-sharing basis. He called himself the Columbus of the social world. Much of Fourier's writing was concerned with human passions, and he computed the optimal size for a community on the basis of a theory of human character combinations: his answer was 1700–1800 people.

A philanthropic landowner at Scâeni, then in Bulgaria, was the first to try out Fourier's scheme, but his neighbors repressed this dangerous idea by force of arms. The concept spread to other parts of the world. In Russia; Fëdor Dostoevski was sentenced to death for belonging to a Fourierist club, although he was reprieved and sent to Siberia instead. Brook Farm in Massachussetts and Red Bank in New Jersey were among several utopian communities in the Fourier style created in the United States.

As the Manuels wryly observed, rural communes had a short life expectancy: "about three years, the span of a serious love affair." But they let their skepticism slip for a moment in noting that Fourier's scheme was never tried exactly as he described, least of all in the matter of a full mix of psychological characters. The Manuels commented:

> And who can say whether his system is not the true balsam for our pains? . . . Fourier's phalanstery has no more been disproved than Plato's Republic.

Notions akin to Fourier's lived on in the kibbutzim of Israel, and in Mahatma Gandhi's ashrams in India. Aldous Huxley and other writers kept returning to the utopian theme of small self-reliant communities. So when the proposition reappeared in 1973 under the title *Small Is Beautiful,* the freshest thing about it was the slogan.

Its British author, Fritz Schumacher, had been an Allied economist in occupied Germany after World War II, and was one of the inventors of the German "economic miracle." He went on to work for Britain's National Coal Board. In both those roles he was quite capable of saying "large is beautiful." But in his famous essays on "economics as if people mattered," published four years before his death, he opted for the small and made it fashionable again among people who worried about the state of the world.

Schumacher rehearsed the salient advantages of small communities. They would assign significant work to everyone, and they would cause less harm to the natural environment than large-scale operations. The finest cities of history were very small by twentieth-century standards. And through a more appropriate scale of operations, the enormous potential of technology and science would fight misery and degradation in intimate contact with actual people: with individuals, families, and small groups, rather than with states and other "abstractions."

Other commentators had reached similar conclusions. The present author had described a decentralized world with a restored wilderness, in *The Environment Game* (1967). The environment eventually hit the covers of *Time, Newsweek,* and *Fortune* in the memorable month of January 1970, and let loose a flood of writings on the theme of ecological societies. Some of these relied on the doubtful authority of a computer at the Massachusetts Institute of Technology, which in *Limits to Growth* (1972) predicted a crash in the human population.

Decentralization was a recurrent theme. The American writer Murray Bookchin declared that "radical agriculture" would restore humanity's sense of community. People would move out from the cities to create ecocommunities tailored artistically to the ecosystems in which they were located and scaled to "human dimensions." Bookchin elaborated these ideas in his book *The Ecology of Freedom* (1981).

By then, questions of size pervaded many people's thinking,

and not just in the counterculture. While dedicated groups of technologists began working on "appropriate" technology for rural communities in the Third World, corporation bosses thought about subdividing their operations into more manageable units. Alvin Toffler in *The Third Wave* (1980) wanted to amend the slogan to "small-within-big is beautiful"; this was retrogressive politically and stylistically. In *Megatrends* (1982), the industrial consultant John Naisbitt perceived a major shift in American attitudes in favor of decentralization. He saw rural areas and small towns booming at the expense of the cities, and neighborhood groups taking many new initiatives. "We are rebuilding from the bottom up," he declared, echoing Gandhi.

The "small-is-beautiful" mainstream, American style, flowed through the writings of Kirkpatrick Sale: *Human Scale* (1980) and *Dwellers in the Land* (1985). The first title related to the use by architects of such measuring units as the length of the forearm or the stride, and design proportions that took account of the human body. Sale wanted the same principle of the human scale to govern town planning, and all other aspects of human life as well:

> Social arrangements, economic conditions, and political structures, even educational and leisure facilities could be designed so that individuals could take in their experience whole and coherently, relate with other people freely and honestly, comprehend all that goes on in their working and civic lives, share in the decisions that make everything function, and not feel intimidated or rendered impotent by large, hidden forces beyond their control or reckoning.

Subtitled *The Bioregional Vision,* Sale's *Dwellers in the Land* offered a poetic synthesis of thinking about ecological solutions to modern problems. Bioregionalism meant, in essence, understanding "the place where we live." Soil, rocks, waters, winds, living things, and the cycle of the seasons: these were things that everyone needed to know. Social and economic arrangements had to adapt to geomorphic ones, in communities typically numbering 5000 to 10,000 people and constrained by the carrying capacity of the land.

Sale was much cooler about technology than Schumacher had been, and vehemently blamed the "scientific worldview" for most of the world's troubles. Even so, he was enthusiastic about a piece of that "worldview": the Gaia hypothesis. This idea was published by the British analytical chemist James Lovelock in 1979, who named it for the Greek Earth goddess. The living organisms of the planet, led by the bacteria, functioned as a coherent system that unconsciously maintained the conditions necessary for life, in much the same way as a living organism regulates its internal functions. This hypothesis was a rational interpretation of atmospheric chemistry and was fraught with practical implications. The mud of estuaries, for example, turned out to be home for many of Gaia's key workers; and if you wanted to create a durable space colony, you had better take a zoo of microbes with you.

While Lovelock went on to make Gaia more mathematical, metaphysical interpretations ascribing consciousness to Gaia abounded in the counterculture. The new cult of Nature-worship (made explicit in *Dwellers in the Land*) gave reverence to the Earth goddess. If "she" was a mnemonic for the indispensable intricacies of planetary biochemistry and biophysics, all well and good. But the latest breed of Nature-worshipers seemed to want to copulate with Gaia and sprawl all over "her," which was technically quite the wrong idea. A true admirer of Gaia would leave her to get on with her biochemical artwork in peace, and the way to do that was to use the best technology available to reduce to a minimum the human demands on the land.

Wearing his economist's hat, Schumacher had defined the appropriate level of capital investment for "small-is-beautiful" technology. It should on no account exceed a year's earnings for each worker, otherwise all the old troubles associated with concentrations of wealth would reappear, including unemployment. So cheapness was a prime requirement for the methods and equipment for the new era. Others were that the technology should be suitable for small-scale application and compatible with the human need for creativity. Schumacher's hopes for such an economy were decidedly low-key. To satisfy human social-psychological needs and reduce the tensions that caused strife and war, economic expectations had to be moderated. Schumacher liked to quote Gandhi: "Earth provides enough for every man's needs, but not for every man's greed."

Greed was by definition excessive, but there were objections to Schumacher's prescriptions of restraint. Politically it was unlikely that any group, except perhaps conscience-stricken affluent people in the Western world, would accept austerity as an objective. Only among some of those who had already benefited to the point of satiation was "growth" a dirty word. Self-betterment was a powerful human motive under any social or political system, and to call it greed would be a needless brake on creativity.

The most serious objection concerned the Third World. Economic growth on a stupendous scale was still required to bring the majority of the world's population even to a standard of living that the better-off minority would regard as marginally acceptable. Those who craved the "economics of permanence" or a "sustainable world," based on low or zero economic growth, seemed too often to be wanting to pull up the ladder and leave the peasants in their medieval pit. The Earth resounded to the chatter of the well-to-do preaching the virtues of poverty to the poor.

The exciting news of the 1980s for would-be utopians was that biotechnology opened the prospect of green machines that met all of Schumacher's criteria for "small-is-beautiful" technology, but without severe limitations on economic growth. They promised to be exactly as he required, cheap, small-scale, and "compatible with man's need for creativity." Yet they were also capable of supporting high and rising standards of living, even taking account of the expected growth of the world's population. By rejecting austerity as a goal and offering a more acceptable economic contract, the high-technology version of "small-is-beautiful" became plausible for ordinary people.

Politics was something else. The big landowners in Bulgaria used firearms to extinguish the first Fourierian agricultural cooperative. In the late twentieth century, too, powerful interests were vested in the status quo. Opponents to the creation of a world of self-reliant villages would include ambitious politicians of nearly all political persuasions, who wanted a national stage to prance on. These would be supported by bureaucrats and military chiefs, by bankers and corporation men, and by trade-union leaders whose livelihoods depended on workers continuing to act like proles.

The miniature navy of the Greenpeace movement joined battle with formidable groups of that kind, in confrontations about whaling, sealing, radioactive-waste disposal, and nuclear-weapons tests. The French secret service went to the trouble of sinking *Rainbow Warrior* in Auckland harbor in 1985, killing the ship's photographer. In some countries, other campaigners slowed down the development of civil nuclear power plants—although this was not necessarily in the best interest of the natural environment. On the whole the green utopians were too tenderhearted to present any serious challenge to authority, and nonviolence was an explicit aim of Schumacher and many others.

In *Dwellers in the Land,* Kirkpatrick Sale answered his own question, "How do we get from this world to that?" by specifying a political movement. This would be akin to some sixty existing "bioregional" groups already at work in the U.S., and also to the Green political parties active in eleven Western European countries, in Australia, and in Japan. The movement would work by educational and reshaping processes that would be necessarily slow and methodical. Although he rejected pacifism and visualized that the "bioregions" would eventually defend themselves with armies in the Swiss style, Sale did not condone rebellion. Indeed he declared: "One cannot imagine bioregionalism being installed by revolution, no matter whose revolution it is."

Those who contemplated the full panoply of the nation-state with its prisons and armies, its stockpiles of nuclear weapons, and its capacity to engineer Big Brother Machines and Doomsday Machines to defend its power and wealth, were entitled to think anything less than a revolution entirely futile. Had the world really changed that much since the czarist police arrested Dostoevski and his friends? And where on Earth was the future in evolving a bioregional paradise only to have it succumb to nuclear winter? A related question was this: Why should American commentators, whose nation-state was created by revolution, find revolutions such a horrifying idea?

The Western liberals remained, though, the doughtiest guardians of the Greek democratic tradition. The Second World War was perceived within the Anglo-American alliance not simply as a struggle for territory among nation-states, but as a crusade against dictatorship. The notion of government by the people would be crucial in any far-reaching decentralization of political power. The Russians and Chinese, in their collective farms and communes run by party trusties, had shown how the trappings of devolution and self-government could be a sham, leaving the real power with the ideologues in the national capitals.

The democratic ideal was always tainted, even in the Western parliaments, by doubts about public competence. Conservative politicians were pessimistic about human nature anyway. Liberals and democratic socialists relied on representative rather than direct democracy to impose their reforms nationwide. The rare instances of direct democracy confirmed the liberals' fears. The people of New Hampshire, setting policies at their town meetings every March, were very grudging of state taxes for welfare and education. And the Swiss were the last people in Europe to grant women the right to vote, in 1971.

Deeper than any arguments about particular policies was the riddle of human nature. Were the ancient Greeks right to imagine that human beings were kindly and reasonable on the whole? Were people fit to govern themselves without national laws and police forces? Given the human capacity for aggression, would a world of separate communities degenerate into endless feuding—Beirut writ large? Biological science was not silent on these questions.

Kropotkin's Sociobiology

In 1882 a Russian prince in exile stood in the aquarium on the seafront at Brighton in England, gazing in wonder as clumsy Molucca crabs tried to assist one of their number that had fallen on its back in a corner of the tank.

> Its comrades came to the rescue, and for one hour's time I watched how they endeavoured to help their fellow-prisoner. They came two at once, pushed their friend from beneath, and after strenuous efforts succeeded in lifting it upright; but then the iron bar would prevent them from achieving the work of rescue, and the crab would again heavily fall upon its back. After many attempts, the helpers would go to the depth of the tank and bring two other crabs, which would begin with fresh forces the same pushing and lifting of their helpless comrade. We stayed in the Aquarium for more than two hours and, when leaving, we again came to cast a glance upon the tank: the work of rescue continued!

For Prince Peter Kropotkin, this was just one example of the cooperative propensity of many animal species, including human beings, which sustained his belief in anarchism. Although it was a far cry from *Limulus* crabs to the desperate deeds of anarchist revolutionaries, Kropotkin was a scientist anxious to find a biological underpinning for his political convictions.

Tuberculosis killed Kropotkin's mother when he was three years old; otherwise he might have lived the conventional life of an aristocrat in czarist Russia. Growing up with a tyrannical father and an unloving stepmother, young Peter Kropotkin and his brother Alexander found affection and high spirits among the serfs of the family estate, although the brothers were forbidden to fraternize with the servants. As a result, Peter Kropotkin saw, through the serfs' eyes, the cruel feudalism that gave his father the power to have his servants whipped, compulsorily mated like cattle, and sent on unreasonably arduous journeys in the depths of the Russian winter. The two young princes, descendants of the first rulers of Russia, became scientists and revolutionaries.

While Alexander finished up as a convict in Siberia and eventually shot himself, Peter made a daring escape from prison in St. Petersburg in 1876. He was then thirty-three years old, and he spent the next forty years of his life in exile in Western Europe, where he was recognized as the greatest libertarian writer of his time. In a letter to George Woodcock, the historian of anarchism, George Bernard Shaw described him in glowing terms: "Personally Kropotkin was amiable to the point of saintliness, and with his full beard and loveable expression might have been a shepherd from the Delectable Mountains."

It was on other mountains that Kropotkin's scientific reputation rested. During service in the czar's army, he had delineated the mountain ranges of Siberia; he also investigated climatic changes during the ice ages and in the desiccation of the steppes that drove the Huns into China and Europe. To become a prophet of anarchism, Kropotkin sacrificed his professional science. He also resisted a temptation to settle down as a watchmaker in the Jura of Switzerland, in a community that practiced exactly the freedom and mutual aid that he was to advertise in his books.

Kropotkin gathered data about German potato fields, French market gardens, and English dairy farms to consider possible yields per acre, exactly as biodynamic gardeners and green engineers were to be doing eighty years later. Intensive agriculture, producing on 1 acre what 50 used to supply, was for him the key to revolution, first to feed the masses during the revolution, and then to create the desired realm of industrial villages where people would divide their working time between fields and factories.

> If you call to your aid science and technical invention. . . . you will be astonished at the facility with which you can bring a rich and varied food out of the soil. . . . Have the factory and the workshop at the gates of your fields and gardens.

Kropotkin's horticultural vision failed to cure the reputation of anarchists more concerned with the apocalyptic destruction of the existing social order. In vain Kropotkin remonstrated with the psychotic terrorists who gave anarchism a thoroughly bad name. Nevertheless, in his essays, lectures, and books, Kropotkin made the idea of living without rulers intellectually respectable.

He was feted at the Finland Station on his return to his homeland, in the interregnum between the Liberal revolution of March 1917 and the Bolshevik revolution of October. He detested "authoritarian" communism and was not surprised when the anarchists were persecuted as thoroughly by the Bolshevik state as they had been by the czarist police. In a "Letter to the Workers of the World," in November 1920, three months before his death, Kropotkin called for an end to the interventionist war against Russia, but he also denounced Lenin's regime. He contrasted the revolutionary situation with what he as an anarchist still dreamed of: a union of free communes, based on the willing collaboration of human brainpower.

> To sweep away that collaboration and to trust to the genius of party dictators is to destroy all the independent nuclei, such as trade unions and the local distributive cooperative organizations, turning them into the bureaucratic organs of the party, as is being done now. But this is the way *not* to accomplish the Revolution; the way to render its realization impossible. [Quoted in George Woodcock, *Anarchism* (1962).]

At the core of all anarchist theory was the belief that human beings were well-behaved by nature and could conduct their affairs in a friendly and orderly manner without supervision. As Kropotkin put it:

> It is not love and not even sympathy upon which Society is based in mankind. It is the conscience—be it only at the stage of an instinct—of human solidarity. It is the unconscious recognition of the force that is borrowed by each man from the practice of mutual aid; of the close dependency of everyone's happiness upon the happiness of all; and of the sense of justice, equity, which brings the individual to consider the rights of every other individual as equal to his own.

Kropotkin was a premature sociobiologist. His book *Mutual Aid: A Factor of Evolution* (1902) was a study in animal behavior, extending to the human domain. He reacted vehemently against the Social Darwinists, including the great Thomas Huxley, who saw in Darwin's "struggle for existence" support for reactionary and pessimistic ideas about humankind. For Huxley, primitive human beings were adapted by nature to "a continuous free fight." Inspired by his own observations of fallow deer and other species coping with the harsh winters of northern Asia, as well as by the crabs in the Brighton aquarium, Kropotkin pointed to collaboration between individuals within animal species ranging from the social insects to birds of prey and monkeys. He went on to cite archeological and anthropological evidence for the coherence and orderliness of primitive tribes. The latter part of *Mutual Aid* was a recital of historical instances of self-government, from the guilds of medieval Europe to the Victorian clubs of bicyclists and mountaineers.

Later evolutionary theorists had a hard time trying to reconcile the Darwinian principle of evolution by natural selection with the evident capacity for altruism and self-denial exhibited both by animals and by human beings. Critics of the resulting sociobiology did not appreciate the strength of the tide of selfishness running through evolution; in this the Social Darwinists had a point. The technical question was how unselfishness and restraint could serve the selfish purposes of the genes.

Tit for Tat

The biological picture was confused for a while by the writings of Konrad Lorenz in Germany, who asserted that human beings were more aggressive and selfish than other animals. This was based on a gross overestimate of the inhibitions that prevent animals of the same species from killing one another. Even as Lorenz's *On Aggression* was being hailed as one of the most important books of the 1960s, observers of animal behavior in the wild were reporting killings among lions, monkeys, hippopotamuses, and gulls, that destroyed his premise. For the evolutionary theorists the problem of aggression was inverted. They had first to find reasons for the inhibitions among animals, and go on to explain especially strong antihomicidal and cooperative tendencies among human beings. Only then would they be ready to address the distinctively human forms of aggression, as in organized crime and warfare.

The first technical breakthrough came in 1964 when William Hamilton of London University offered a theory of "kin selection," such that altruism shown to near-relatives could favor the survival of one's own genes. This explained rather precisely the patterns of cooperation observed in ants and other animal species, but when applied to human beings it predicted intensely tribal behavior. Warfare between groups, territoriality, slavery, and cruelty and deceit of many kinds all emerged as "natural" phenomena in Hamilton's theory.

Although human beings had lived in more or less isolated family tribes during most of their evolutionary history, they often fought within families and tribes, and yet could cooperate with completely unrelated people, even to the point of risking their lives to save a stranger. In 1971, Robert Trivers of Harvard University offered a genetic theory of "reciprocal altruism," based on a system of give-and-take between nonrelatives, such that I might do you a service in the expectation that some day you may reciprocate and aid the survival of myself or a close relative of mine. This was a pattern of behavior that might evolve most readily in a species like that of human beings, having long memories and a capacity for calculation. The inherent selfishness of the genes was thus mitigated by "enlightened self-interest," which was no sentimental matter of brotherly or sisterly love but a tough-minded, calculating mode of life, evidently reinforced by strong feelings about fairness, guilt, and virtue.

The theory of games loomed large in Trivers' work, and in that of other evolutionary biologists trying to understand the behavior of animals and human beings. John Maynard Smith of the University of Sussex demonstrated, in 1974, how game theory could help in understanding conflict and the resolution of conflict among animals. Fighting between animals of the same species was typically a matter of ritual snarls, gestures, and token bites, and if it should escalate beyond that stage, one party or the other would usually break off the fight. In a simplistic view of evolution, a more ruthless animal might be expected to prevail over its associates of the same species, and to leave more surviving offspring, which would carry the genes predisposing to "hawkish" behavior. Maynard Smith showed how, on the contrary, restrained behavior could be an "evolutionary stable strategy."

Treating the contests between pairs of animals as games, Maynard Smith considered five possible strategies for animals, to which he gave nicknames. "Doves" fought in a restrained, conventional manner and retreated if the opponent escalated the fight; "hawks" escalated the fight at once and went on regardless; "bullies" escalated too, but retreated if the opponent also escalated; "probers" fought conventionally but escalated if the opponent also fought conventionally; "retaliators" fought conventionally unless the opponent escalated the fight, in which case they did likewise.

By assigning scores to the outcome of fights between any pair of opponents, Maynard Smith deduced that the last of the list, the "retaliators," had the best, evolutionary stable strategy. It prevented the subjugation that more timid behavior would attract, while avoiding the injuries that aggressive fighters would suffer when faced with a group of resolute "retaliators." This was the first persuasive explanation of how ritualized fighting evolved among animal species.

The game that attracted most scientific interest among evolutionists and psychologists was the Prisoner's Dilemma. The name came from a story about two prisoners, separately interrogated, who could either support each other's story, or default by confessing to the crime and giving evidence against the other. In its simplest formulation, each of two players could elect to cooperate or default. If both cooperated, both scored positively, but only a little. If both defaulted, both lost a little. If one offered cooperation while the other defaulted, the first lost heavily and the other scored high. Trivers used this game in developing his theory of reciprocal altruism.

The Prisoner's Dilemma yielded to no mathematical analysis, but in 1981 Robert Axelrod and William Hamilton (by then at the University of Michigan) reported long series of the game, played by computer, which established the best strategy. This too turned out to be a retaliator strategy, or "Tit for Tat": offer cooperation, but if the other player defaults, then default yourself in the following round. In human terms, "retaliate, but bear no grudge."

Simple, abstract games were not to be confused with real life. Two-player games played in long series were different from a one-off version of the same game, or similar games involving large numbers of players. The possibility of players making mistakes could also exert a profound effect. Even at the theoretical level the winning strategy for the long-series Prisoner's Dilemma game was not an evolutionary stable strategy in Maynard Smith's sense. A group of animals that evolved to cooperate by a "Tit for Tat" strategy was vulnerable to infiltration by mutants that seemed to be similar, in always offering cooperation at the first encounter, but then they unexpectedly defaulted at a later stage. "One may smile, and smile, and be a villain."

The theorists were slowly making sense of the evolution of cooperative versus competitive behavior. It was applicable to any species, as Kropotkin would have wished, and even to interactions between species, such as the symbiosis of nitrogen-fixing bacteria with bean plants. Prudent biologists were cautious about drawing strong inferences concerning human social behavior from work in progress. If the eventual outcome was going to be some definitive account of human nature, it was likely to contradict some long-cherished political and religious beliefs. The stakes were extremely high, and scientific caution and skepticism correspondingly strong.

Had Kropotkin himself lived to see the flowering of sociobiology, he would have been fascinated by the vast amount of new knowledge about social behavior in animals. Game theory analyzed vigilance in birds, and defined how much time feeding birds should spend looking out for predators on behalf of their group—the "voluntary sentries" that Kropotkin himself observed by the Siberian lakes. The elements of selfishness, calculation, and violence inherent in modern sociobiology would not have disturbed Kropotkin nearly as much as they upset tender-minded sociologists unwilling to grant that the very existence of human societies required biological explanations in terms of life and death.

Kropotkin acknowledged the competition for food among animals of the same species, and cannibalism and headhunting among human tribes. A human capacity for injustice was manifest in the social order to the overthrow of which Kropotkin devoted all his energies. He accepted the prospect of violent revolution, because he did not expect the privileged minority to give up its privileges bloodlessly, although he wanted to minimize the number of victims and the bitterness.

The "retaliator" strategy identified by Maynard Smith as the evolutionary stable strategy for restrained fighting among animals might have struck Kropotkin forcibly. The strategy owed its strength not to the ferocity of individuals, but to the readiness of ordinary "well-behaved" animals to curb hawkish or bullying behavior whenever it cropped up in maverick individuals. But retaliation implied a capacity for violence in the ordinary animals. If Kropotkin's ghost reasoned with that, he might find his confidence waning about the tranquility of his communes.

The innate aggressiveness that human beings shared with most other animals was neither the "death wish" of the Freudians, nor the irreducible drive described by Lorenz. Edward Wilson of Harvard University likened it to a "mix of chemicals ready to be transformed by specific catalysts that are added, heated, and stirred at some later time." (*On Human Nature*, 1978.) He declared that people were genetically predisposed toward learning some form of communal aggression; the form was influenced by the group's circumstances and needs, and also by its previous history. Issues of territory and property loomed large among these human environmental factors.

Antagonism between groups was illuminated also by social psychology. A succession of experiments, in the U.S., Britain and elsewhere, demonstrated people's alacrity in identifying with any group or team to which they were assigned, however arbitrarily. This entailed an almost automatic tendency to favor the in-group, while disparaging out-groups. The team spirit was indispensable to all kinds of cooperative enterprises within a group and was the underpinning of Kropotkin's "mutual aid." But it could be as easily channeled into aggression toward other groups, by demagogues and military officers.

The practical questions concerning a world of villages created by some social or political revolution, were (1) whether people would spontaneously organize sensible autonomous social systems as Kropotkin expected, and (2) whether the villages would live at peace with one another. Tentative answers based on the slowly unfolding theoretical knowledge of human nature, and on the archeological and anthropological evidence, were these:

(1) Yes, stable systems of self-government would emerge quickly within most villages, provided they were large enough. There would be a spontaneous access of loyalty to each village and its customs. But making it democratic would demand great vigilance, designed especially to spot and control the aggressive male seeking to become dictator, chief, high priest, or tyrant, as the Greeks had called him. There would, though, be mutual aid in plenty. Some communities might well achieve the anarchistic communism of which Kropotkin dreamed, although this would be only one form of government among many.

(2) No, peace between villages could not be guaranteed. Maximizing their dispersal and self-reliance would minimize the risk of petty conflicts over territory and resources, but rivalries would always be latent. If there really were a million autonomous villages, the extraordinary variety of social and political systems emerging among them would be bound to include authoritarian, militaristic, or religious groups lusting for empires or souls. These would be like cancer cells threatening the tissue of villages, and would have to be checked. And wherever several rival groups of that kind existed close together, the scene would indeed be a rural version of Beirut.

The abolition of nation-states might bring many benefits, but even the incomplete scientific assessments of human nature and social systems already showed that there would be no escape from politics and strife. Each human being was a bag of inseparable contradictions: altruism and selfishness, cruelty and gentleness, logic and passion, light and darkness, and all social systems were open to abuse.

In *Of the Social Contract* (1762), Jean-Jacques Rousseau set out guiding principles for a democratic city, but he had difficulty with the crucial distinction between the will of all (consensus) and simple majority rule, which could harm minorities and individuals. When Kenneth Arrow, in the twentieth century, offered axioms concerning collective decision making, he set in train work by social mathematicians which proved that a perfect system was impossible. You could not at one and the same time have collective decisiveness and equality of power.

Such conclusions were not what the utopian dreamers wanted to hear. They craved a formula that would rid the world of iniquity and inequity, and for some of them nonviolence was the first priority. Curiously many of those who most abhorred the blatant aggression of imperial conquests, organized crime, and nuclear arsenals, were the keenest to deny any human tendency toward aggressiveness. This was typical of the intellectual oddities of the late twentieth century.

Under Western Skulls

Public-television executives in New York objected to the title of a program made by the BBC: *The Violent Universe.* The program told of certain discoveries by astronomers that revealed, in the serene-looking night sky, cataclysms of imploding stars and exploding galaxies. These hinted at the existence of black holes, the most destructive objects ever to enter the human imagination. Other observations confirmed that the universe originated in a Big Bang, and suggested it would end in a Big Crunch. To call that violent seemed no flight of fancy, but the TV people were quite anxious about doing so. They feared that telling the public they lived in a violent universe would encourage violence in the streets. After a controversy about whether descriptions of events thousands or billions of light-years away had any close bearing on race relations in American cities, reason prevailed and the title stayed. This trivial dispute gave an unexpected glimpse under Western skulls.

The churchmen who, 400 years earlier, opposed the idea of the Earth orbiting around the sun were a standing joke for twentieth-century folk who found amusement in hindsight. Yet the theory of Copernicus was a grave matter for those responsible for millions of immortal souls. They had come to depend on Nature's display of hierarchical perfection in the sky as a model for the relationship of angels, bishops, peasants, and earwigs. Scientific assaults on the model threatened the religious system itself.

By the middle of the twentieth century educated people in the Western world had a quite different model of Nature. It reinforced their philosophical beliefs about progress. But subsequent scientific findings destroyed the picture of "progressive" Nature as comprehensively as Kepler and Galileo disposed of the old hierarchy in the solar system. This scientific revolution was greeted with much the same dismay and opposition as the Copernican revolution, and many people were unwilling to register the signals.

The belief was that God voted for the Democrats. The mild programs of persistent reform favored by Western liberals were thought to be clearly mirrored in Nature's own policies. On its safe platform in the universe, life evolved slowly but surely over billions of years. The arrow of progress was onward and upward to better adapted, cleverer, and nicer organisms, capable of grieving over their martinis for the latest famine victims, while sending young men to stamp out the forest fires of misguided revolution. Nature smiled on the human species as its finest creation to date and blessed it with the best of all possible worlds.

Maybe not quite the best. H-bombs were a disagreeable necessity, and the catalogs of endangered species and eroded soils made embarrassing reading. Never mind: If we listened carefully we would hear the voices of beings even nobler than ourselves, beings inhabiting the planets of other stars. With millions of extra years of evolution under their belts, they would be formidably wise, and they would teach us the ways of righteousness and peace.

The picture of gradual evolution in a stable environment, which had become for some a surrogate for God, was blotted out by a quick-fire succession of discoveries between 1960 and 1985. Unwittingly, all the sciences ganged up against those who thought that Nature was benign. The turmoil among distant stars and galaxies was the least of it, because the sun at least was stable and the stars threatened life on Earth only if a supernova should explode uncomfortably close.

More to the point was the discovery in the 1960s that the continents were adrift, and that mountain ranges were the products of traffic accidents. The volcanoes and earthquakes that routinely killed thousands of people at a stroke were not regrettable flaws in Nature's scheme; they were intrinsic to the machinery of plates that created the continents and renewed the oceans. The chroniclers of life on Earth had to reinterpret their fossils to take account of the continents barging around like so many Noah's Arks.

The climate too turned out to be unreliable. The old table of about four ice ages in the recent geological past, with long warm interglacials between them, was replaced by a graph showing dozens of oscillations and fluctuations. Most of these could be explained by inevitable alterations of the Earth's posture in orbit, and the message was that the next ice age was pending. When it came with its ice sheets and droughts it would destroy forests more thoroughly and alter the carbon-dioxide content of the air more drastically than the most ruthless industrialists.

Discoveries concerning the mechanisms of evolution were even more disconcerting. Evolutionary biologists cherished a neo-Darwinian picture in which natural selection, acting in a patiently creative manner, continuously refined the plants and beasts to suit their environments. It snuffed out harmful mutations, while favoring mutations that offered new advantages in life. Every change had a meaning and, in some poetic or para-religious sense, a purpose.

Molecular biologists threw the first paint pot at this portrait of smiling Nature. Detailed comparisons of genes and their products in different species revealed that most evolutionary changes were a matter of chance, involving neutral mutations that neither helped nor harmed their possessors. Being unable to express an opinion for or against them, natural selection lost its grip on the destiny of species. Traditional evolutionists were outraged. If this were so, they cried, evolution would have hardly any meaning and would not be going anywhere in particular. Exactly.

Next to be defaced was the idea of gradualism. In the specific matter of the evolution of the human species, biologists of the old school wanted to grant Nature as long as possible for creating its masterpiece, yet comparisons of molecules revealed that the prehuman lineage separated from the apes only a few million years ago. Across all the lineages of life, gradual evolution had always been a weak hypothesis because intermediate forms between one species and the next were hard to find among the fossils. Tough-minded paleontologists said that the fossil record ought to be interpreted at face value, which meant the abrupt replacement of one species by the next. They were condemned as heretics and revolutionists.

When the marvelous little robot spacecraft nosed around other planets of the solar system, scientists made two salutary discoveries. The first was that Mars was a lifeless desert—a matter of keen disappointment to those whose evolutionary perspective required that life should originate and survive wherever possible. The other discovery was that all of the harder planets and moons were disfigured, like the Earth's moon, with scars, in the form of huge craters, from impacts of comets or asteroids. The solar system was not the orderly or peaceful setting for life that many people had imagined.

The shocks to the old order culminated in the discovery, circa 1980, that the dinosaurs were wiped out by a comet or asteroid hitting the Earth. The new images of the violent universe and quirky evolution merged into a stereoscopic whole. It soon became plain that such impacts had afflicted the Earth many times, causing explosions equivalent to billions of H-bombs going off. On one such occasion, some 245 million years ago, 96 percent of all species of marine animals were annihilated. By 1985, investigators of these catastrophes had dubbed the resulting barren seas the "Strangelove Ocean."

In further unserene serendipity, scientists studying the effects of nuclear war found parallels for the nuclear winter in the ancient impact events. Particularly striking, and drawing all the new horror stories together, was a report from the University of Chicago in 1985, that a thin deposit of soot coincided with the extinction of the dinosaurs. Nature burned the Earth's forests in its casual game of cometary billiards, and except in the labored manner of its contrivance, nuclear winter had not even the merit of originality.

In the short interval that separated the reigns of Eisenhower and Reagan, Khrushchev and Gorbachev, Elvis Presley and Bruce Springsteen, Nature had been unmasked as a reckless engineer. If one had to be anthropomorphic about it, Nature was more interested in what could be done with black holes or bulldozing glaciers than in the welfare of fragile genes and organisms. There was some consolation from the Gaia hypothesis: the worldwide conspiracy of organisms contrived to maintain livable conditions despite all these drastic events. Its author doubted, though, if the Gaian system could go on working indefinitely on a geological timescale.

Life progressed (if that was still the appropriate verb) by accident, and species and ecosystems established over millions of years could be eliminated at a stroke. For anyone rash enough to model their ideas of human social progress on analogies with natural evolution, this was all bad news. Marxists were as much confounded as the Western liberals. So too were those on the Far Right who drew encouragement from evolutionary notions about "the survival of the fittest." If Nature had any leanings at all analogous to human politics, it was an anarchist.

The Copernican revolution that bothered the bishops had no bearing on the merits of the teachings of Jesus. The Copernican-like revolution in natural philosophy in the late twentieth century left the substantive issues of political choices and human progress almost exactly where they were before. Yet it entailed a psychological shift that was relevant to the theme of green machines and the future of human society. When false natural analogs had been ruled out of order, the home truths for nice guys were mainly negative.

Ecological activists could no longer claim that "Nature knows best." Nor could they suggest, as some had tried to do, that human beings were not in charge of the planet. On the contrary, they were a peculiar dominant species put here in a typical fit of aberration by Nature itself. They lacked the wit until late in the day to see what harm they might be doing to the animals and plants they loved. With a new sense of responsibility, engineers were already sketching plans to use space missiles with H-bombs to destroy any wayward asteroid that threatened to send us (and the elephants and tigers too) to the same mass grave as the dinosaurs. These were true servants of Gaia, who saw how "she" was embroiled in Nature's self-destructive wars.

In the political mainstream, Marxists were not entitled to assert that their revolutions were the necessary fulfilment of the scientific laws of progress; there were no such laws. Nor, on the other hand, had Western liberals any right to rule out revolution on evolutionary grounds. There were plenty of good human reasons for arguing that revolutions typically replaced one gang of rogues by another at a terrible cost in human life. But the scientific study of Nature gave no sanctification for the belief that gradual reforms would work out fine in the end; still less for telling ordinary people to abide by the law, sit on their hands, and watch their children die.

The Swiss Model

Especially obnoxious in the view of American liberals were their compatriots who subscribed to a monthly magazine called *Soldier of Fortune* and spent a lot of their time practicing on shooting ranges with shotguns, pistols, and semiautomatic rifles. Their politics typically made Ronald Reagan seem like a socialist, and their special heroes were the Green Berets of the Vietnam War. More than a decade after the defeat of the number-one superpower by a bunch of Indo-Chinese peasants, they harbored special resentment for "Hanoi Jane" Fonda and the television networks, which, in the opinion of this fraternity, broke the Americans' will to win.

In company with the National Rifle Association, the Soldiers of Fortune bitterly opposed any attempts by lawmakers to discourage men from keeping rifles and pistols in their homes. A British journalist, Simon Hoggart of *The Observer,* was startled to find them wearing battle fatigues in the hotel lobby during a convention in Las Vegas, Nevada. He reported that they were "waiting for the day when the Russians rolled over the U.S. border."

At an intercontinental ballistic missile's throw from the U.S., in the Alpine valleys of Europe, the Swiss Rifle Association had a membership of nearly 600,000. This was unsurprising when you knew that every healthy Swiss man was required by law to keep an automatic rifle or a pistol at home, and to practice regularly in a shooting club. The Swiss men also dressed up to take part in annual marching and skiing competitions in full battle gear. To make up for a scarcity of real wars, they fought mock battles with live ammunition. They were waiting for the day when the Russians rolled over the Swiss border.

As industrious and peace-loving people, the Swiss ranked high in any liberal gazetteer of admirable nations, yet their menfolk were more militaristic in their habits and traditions than any others in the Western world. What political relativity made it admirable that every Swiss farmer or clerk or schoolteacher should have a gun in his closet and keep verifying his ability to kill with it, while Americans doing the same thing at their own expense seemed to be homicidal crackpots?

That was the trouble about young men with guns: it was hard to tell the Good Guys from the Bad. A standard television image of the 1980s showed indistinguishable boys with Kalashnikovs taking potshots at each other across the streets of Beirut. All were despicable terrorists and brave freedom fighters, in the eyes of different onlookers. Judgments took account of a spectrum of nuances that ranged from superpower geopolitics to local concern about women and children.

Most nation-states passed through a Beirut phase, and by retrospective definition, the Good Guys always won. At the time, it never seemed as simple as that, and they were often vilified up to their moment of triumph. The only logic that ever came into it was the willingness of young men to kill or be killed for a cause in which they believed. The outcome of the battle determined whether they were buried like heroes or dogs.

If Switzerland was the model for a peaceful and prosperous world of villages, it had to be taken literally. Power to the people was assured by a military alliance of cantons that began in the mountains south of Zurich for the defiance of a German king. What kept the Swiss neutral from 1515 onward, and secure within their borders even when encircled by the Axis powers in 1940 to 1944, was the same military tradition. To try to borrow the Swiss blessings of devolution and peace without the aid of guns would be like hoping to grow corn without seeds.

People went about their daily business with expressions as calm as the cows of the Emmental. If you looked hard, you would find 3500 professional soldiers in Switzerland. But if you were rash enough to try to invade the country you would find every bridge and road tunnel mined for demolition, and concealed artillery shooting at you. Out of the valleys and hills would appear, by instant magic, an army of 625,000 men.

With twelve front-line divisions the Swiss order of battle was comparable with the West German peacetime army, the largest in Western Europe, despite the fact that the West German population and defense expenditure were both ten times greater than Switzerland's. There was some saving in tanks, because Switzerland's mountainous terrain was better suited to infantry and ski troops than to armored divisions, but more than 300 combat aircraft gave the Swiss one of the more powerful air forces in Western Europe. Many of the fighters were kept hidden in caves in the mountainsides.

Military strength out of all proportion to the size of the country flowed from the fact that four out of five Swiss men were part-time soldiers between the ages of twenty and fifty, or fifty-five in the case of officers. Conscientious objection to military service was punished by some months in prison. The youngest men belonged to elite mobile formations of the *Auszug,* and those selected for promotion had to give up more time for military training. At the age of thirty-three, the men transferred to the *Landwehr,* a chain of twenty-three brigades responsible for static defense of frontiers and redoubts. The forty-three to fifty-year-olds made up the *Landsturm,* based in home territory to defend the civilian population. The Swiss troops were taught that, if their main formations were broken, they were to continue fighting stubbornly in guerrilla fashion, taking advantage of terrain that they knew far better than any invader. The aim was to make the "admission charge" to Switzerland unacceptably high. The appointment of a commander-in-chief in time of danger was one of the few tasks entrusted to the country's Federal Assembly.

Yeats's idea that every person was king or queen took legal

form in Switzerland. The sovereign was the voice of the people, expressed in local and cantonal votes and in federal referenda and initiatives. When some men went to vote they wore swords—medieval signs that linked the right to vote with the willingness to fight. The automatic rifle in the closet, complete with its ammunition in a sealed box, remained the symbol of sovereignty. How many of the world's heads of state would sleep quietly if their people were so armed?

Some Europeans in the North Atlantic Treaty Organization wished they had the Swiss system instead of a strategy that outfaced the massed tanks of the Warsaw Pact with a "deep-strike" strategy backed by nuclear weapons. For a purely defensive "high-admission-charge" strategy, other countries lacked the natural fortresses of the "Tibet of Europe," but rapid developments in military sensors and high-precision missiles were favoring defenders over attackers. Weapons that reliably destroyed tanks and aircraft were becoming far cheaper than the tanks and aircraft themselves.

Nuclear weapons (*pace* Star Wars) remained the great exception against which there was no reliable defense. But here too there was a Swiss model to be taken literally. Every modern house in Switzerland had a nuclear shelter in its basement—not a mere fallout screen but a concrete bunker with a massive sealed door, capable of withstanding a 1-megaton blast at a distance of less than 3 kilometers. Public shelters were hardened to the same standard. Strange to behold were underground hospitals equipped with all the gadgets of modern medicine and surgery, but in the hope that they would never have to accept a single patient.

These precautions far surpassed those of nuclear-armed states as well as of others, all of which appeared much higher than Switzerland on the target lists for nuclear weapons. Yet those other countries made exceptional arrangements to conduct their rulers to safety in airborne headquarters or deep bunkers, while leaving the people to face the music. The difference was that in Switzerland the people were still the kings and queens.

POST-SCRIPT | THE WINTER FARMS

THE rumor that ran among the ordinary inhabitants of the planet Earth was that men of unbelievable wickedness were planning to blot out the sun and starve everyone to death. Cities were no longer possible places to live, because you would be eating rats and your neighbors would be eating you. The pomp of civilization and science brought the human species back in the end to its atavistic fear of cannibalism.

The revolution of the Winter Farms at the end of the twentieth century came about when people moved out of the cities in large numbers, looking for places in the countryside where they and their families might survive the nuclear winter. Very few of them had even heard of Fourier or Kropotkin or the modern prophets of bucolic societies. But the native wit of ordinary human beings, and their talents for bargaining and cooperating, invented a million ad hoc social systems for the Winter Farms. The piecemeal knowledge and skills that individuals brought with them from their lost civilization to the empty fields expressed themselves in the frenzy of creativity that altered the face of the planet. What started as a foxhole and a ramshackle greenhouse could evolve in a decade into a graceful and prosperous microcity.

"With hindsight I could have predicted that," theoretical physicists liked to joke. The startling events that began circa 1990 seemed in retrospect to gush naturally from the pent-up hopes and fears of the previous decade.

The pressure from biotechnology was very hopeful in a material sense. It pushed toward ever higher productivity from the land, and shrewder use of living materials in coherent systems, the green machines. In combination with electronics it made the old dream of small, self-reliant communities attainable, and not austerely but with rising living standards. Information technology could ensure that people living in rural areas need not

THE GREEN MACHINES

feel like country bumpkins. An important characteristic shared
by biotechnology and information technology was that their
production centers as well as their products could be diffused
across the country, away from the old manufacturing centers.

Science planners and industrialists were united in a conviction that biotechnology and information technology would ride
the wave of the next big economic boom. The idea of a fifty-
year "long wave" of booms and slumps, associated with the
name of the Soviet economist Nikolai Kondratieff, was back
in favor in the 1980s, coupled with the expectation that the
next big boom was due to begin in the 1990s. Joseph Schum-
peter of Harvard, Christopher Freeman of the University of
Sussex, and others had developed technological explanations
for the Kondratieff cycles. There were differences of opinion
about cause and effect, but some agreement that each major
boom was associated with the rise of novel industries, whether
railroads and the steel industry in the mid-nineteenth century,
or electronics and synthetic materials a hundred years later.

The puzzle was to tell what human purposes the information
technology and biotechnology of the late twentieth century
would serve, and where the jobs would come from to sustain
the economic surge. People whose business was information
for the public saw market saturation looming even before the
supposed economic takeoff was due to begin. You couldn't eat
or ride a video show. Manufacturing and clerical jobs were
threatened rather than boosted by the rise of computers and
robots. In agricultural biotechnology, too, the main tendency
was toward high productivity, which reduced the number of
jobs on the land.

Also in short supply was the crucial element of fun. Technologies prominent in the four previous booms of the nineteenth
and twentieth centuries had direct appeal to huge consumer
markets. Pretty textiles, railroads, electricity, and cars, all were
fun in their various ways; warfare was always fun to somebody.
Home computers and unlimited electronic communication
promised, at best, lonely kinds of amusement, and it was hard
to see much fun for the consumer in knowing that the plastic
in a bucket was made by microbes instead of chemists.

Technologically, economically, and commercially, any idea

that created a major public demand for biotechnology and electronics would be pushing at an open door. And what could be more fun than creating new lifestyles in a world of villages and equipping them with green machines? Then too, the amount of work waiting to be done would be essentially unlimited, although how it would translate into paid jobs was not always clear. The snag was that a general enthusiasm for green machines on the part of the public was hard to imagine without some extraordinary shift in interests.

For many unemployed young people, who were often the children of those who had been sucked into the industrial cities by the boom of the 1950s, the prospects were grim. Overcapacity and technological obsolescence in the factories, automation in those that survived, and a flight to suburbs by the well-to-do, created ghost towns inhabited by living people. Efficient transport and communications had made many cities superfluous, even without the coup de grace threatened by nuclear weapons. But the poor, including the surplus populations from rural areas, still crowded the cities as if there were safety in numbers. The local booms were in drugs and crime.

The world's farmers too had reached a crisis in their relationships with the rest of the global economy. In the rich countries, overproduction would put many of them out of business unless they could find new uses for their land and their products. In the Third World, continuing population growth intensified the pressure on the land, and the peasants seemed trapped like flies in treacle by a system that gave them little hope that their children would be substantially better off than themselves. Biotechnology threatened to curtail even their modest profits from cash crops, by growing or substituting the products in the industrialized countries.

Like the chorus in a Greek tragedy, worried people chanted that the planet was in a mess. People treated like animals would breed like animals. The tigers and pandas were dying and so were Germany's forests. And what was going to happen when the oil ran out, and when the soil ran out?

One way and another, the world was ready to be turned upside down. It happened when ordinary people recognized that conventional politics, diplomacy, and protest had run out of ideas for preventing a nuclear calamity. They sensed that the policies of a few nations had reduced everyone in the world to the status of hapless peasants—so they had better all start acting like peasants. Economic theory and the rhetoric of partisan politics shrank to zero in the minds of people whose chief wish was to avoid being eaten.

Environmentalists who had preached in an abstract way the virtues of the rural life were horrified to see millions of people who had not even read the lists of endangered species going out unschooled to fend for themselves. The pert comment from the migrants was, "But *we* are the most endangered species." Politicians, bureaucrats, trade-union leaders, bankers, and everyone else with a vested interest in the system of urbanized nation-states said: "You're crazy. You cannot destroy everything our parents and grandparents have created, eliminate jobs, and reduce our great nation to a bunch of peasant communities, all for the sake of an imagined risk." The response was: "Tell that to Washington and Moscow."

Gruesome Arithmetic

When scientists calculated the deaths from starvation after a nuclear war, during their study for SCOPE (Scientific Committee on Problems of the Environment) they made a highly optimistic assumption about the feeding arrangements. When they had arrived at an estimate of what food would be available in various countries after a nuclear winter and the consequent loss of harvests, they imagined the food stocks being divided in such a way as to keep the maximum number of people alive. This meant allotting a survival ration of 2000 kilocalories a day to one section of the population and no food at all to the rest.

In the case of India, for example, severe climatic effects would reduce the available food to a level where it could, at best, support 10–25 percent of the population. In 1983, the total population was estimated at 725 million. The SCOPE figures meant that roughly 125 million people should receive their 2000 kilocalories a day—not a morsel more nor less—and 600 million would be told to sit down quietly and starve. In human terms this was unjust and totally impracticable, as the scientists knew perfectly well. The trouble with the gruesome arithmetic of nuclear winter was that if the rest of India's population received or seized even small amounts of food, virtually everyone would die.

To be realistic, that was the most likely outcome of severe chilling in India. An occasional food hoarder, cannibal, or soldier who took his food at gunpoint might survive, but to a first approximation, India's population would be annihilated if the season's wheat and rice were lost after a nuclear war. In theory, the rich nuclear-armed states (U.S., U.S.S.R., Britain, and France) would be much better off than the Indians from the point of view of surviving the nuclear winter. If most of their populations died as a result of direct effects of nuclear weapons, the stocks should be sufficient to support the survivors, assuming that food and people could be brought together, and the food shared fairly. Those faring best of all would be the food exporting countries of the Southern Hemisphere, notably Argentina and Australia, and they would in effect inherit the Earth. The climatic effects of a nuclear war fought mainly in the north would be muted in the south, and even if half the harvests were lost, they would still be sufficient to feed the entire populations.

Behind the arithmetic and all the assumptions it contained was a dimly perceived picture of a world brought to chaos by the anarchism of the system of nation-states. But certain images in the picture were very plain. In one, crowds of men, women, and children streaming out of a city in search of food, overwhelmed the farming communities with little advantage to themselves. In another image, a squad of armed soldiers roamed the countryside, taking the food by force, either on its own account or to feed the privileged. It was to avoid the billions of personal tragedies that could result from such circumstances that the Winter Farms were created.

They were also necessary for the long term, looking beyond the first dreadful year to an era when national governments had vanished or lost control, when some smoke of the war might still be persisting and reducing harvests, when transport and public energy supplies were vestigial in most places, and when trade had virtually ceased. Except in a few favored countries far to the south, the only way most people were going to have any serious chance of survival in the aftermath of a nuclear war was by turning their backs on their national leaderships and making their own arrangements.

The chief requirement was to evacuate the cities, not hours before the war, but years. The cities were doomed, either as targets for nuclear weapons or as places incapable of supporting themselves during the nuclear winter. A "save-our-cities" movement, led by property owners and industrialists facing financial ruin, started stockpiling food and setting up green machines on rooftops, walls, and parks. By such means, some much-loved cities survived into the new era, though with reduced populations. Those who left knew that the nuclear targeteers could eliminate any city in the world, even if only out of spite.

The movement out of the cities was gradual, cautious, and extremely varied in its practicalities. When families, community leaders, and businessmen from the cities began visiting the farming villages to talk of settling there, the rural people were at first suspicious and unhelpful. Farmers spoke in bureaucratic terms of land-use planning permission. They were slow to see that these courteous approaches in good time were greatly preferable to hungry hordes appearing on the skyline.

Some well-to-do, well-educated people bought up land to make Winter Farms strictly for their own families and favored friends. The general view was that they had not thought matters through to a post-nuclear world when money would mean nothing and these Yuppy Strangeloves would desperately need help from their neighbors for essential supplies and for defense. But the green machines were available off the shelf for those who could afford them. As early as the mid-1980s, the Institute of Ecotechnics, near Tucson, Arizona was developing a greenhouse living system for ten people and suggesting that it could be adopted as a nuclear-winter shelter.

On a larger and more appropriate scale, entrepreneurs who

read the public mood began to create microcities both as products of their industries and as bases for their factories. They
offered their own work forces and all the supporting tradesmen
and services the prospect of a congenial life in a rural setting,
with built-in safeguards against the nuclear winter. Small country towns with enterprising councils created municipal Winter
Farms. Every initiative gave a boost to the development of
appropriate green machines and also intensified the rumor that
cities were no place to live.

Farmers awoke at last to the fact that land prices were falling
in cities and rising in their own areas. They started doing some
arithmetic in consultation with their neighbors and began ad-
vertising Winter Farms. Those near the cities stressed their
convenience; the inhabitants of more remote areas promised
greater safety. Local actions of this kind, improvised in a million
different ways in rich and poor countries around the world,
assimilated a much larger fraction of the urban populations
than the private, industrial, or municipal Winter-Farm packages.

The legal and financial arrangements varied far more at first
than they did in the end. Needs common to every sizable Winter Farm became apparent, new social and economic systems
emerged, and the incomers outnumbered the indigenous populations. In essence, a person could buy his way into a Winter
Farm with cash, with labor, or with both. At first, many people
reluctant to give up well-paid jobs in the cities simply mailed
their subscriptions to the Winter Farm of their choice, and
unemployed people with skills or muscle power to offer were
taken on to do most of the early work. In some places, archaic
systems of apprenticeship and indentured labor reappeared.
But a great deal of the perfection and embellishment of the
Winter Farms was done voluntarily, with all the satisfaction
of a hobby. Anyone who had a way with microbes or microcomputers could be sure of plenty of fun, and for the rest it was
an endlessly fascinating game of Robinson Crusoe.

Although the transition took twenty years, there was always
a sense of urgency because nuclear winter could strike at any
time. From the outset, provision for survival took priority over
other goals such as economic prosperity and creature comforts

in the newly enlarged rural communities. But gradually, as the best of the Winter Farms achieved a wealthy self-reliance, the centers of gravity of economic activity shifted from the urban to the rural areas. The numbers of jobs in the cities dwindled, and more and more families moved permanently into the countryside.

The old, the sick, and the disabled in the urban areas were in danger of being left to starve. The loss of national and city tax revenues that accompanied the demographic and economic transformation caused a crisis in established welfare systems. The Winter Farms were reluctant to take in unproductive mouths; some even barred children. The solutions that emerged usually relied on people handing over their pensions to the Winter Farms, or on healthy relatives working harder to gain admission for their kin. But in countries where high mobility and divorce had broken family ties, the elderly sometimes died of neglect. And everyone with an infectious disease was left out in the cold. Many latent prejudices about race, religion, and sexual behavior reasserted themselves in the recruiting panels of the Winter Farms. The attempts by the outcasts to make their own shelters and survival systems were pathetic on the whole, but a few were so successful that "normal" people applied to join.

At an early stage many Winter Farms with preconceived ideas of how big they should be turned even young and fit people away. They often regretted it when they found themselves short of particular skills. As the pressure of applicants intensified, communities that had set a target of a few hundred people found themselves with ten times that number. Their confidence grew with their numbers, and as the green machines began to take shape.

Winter Farms that stayed too small and austere often broke up in angry disorder. The reasons were sometimes technical, for example when the systems failed to provide an adequate diet even under normal sunshine. But social and personal factors were more often to blame, and small communities were more likely to produce opinionated cliques and petty dictators. Although Charles Fourier had peculiar theoretical reasons of his own for suggesting a minimum of 1700–1800 people to achieve the right mix of personalities in a community, it turned out to be a good guess. The availability of earmarked land limited the scale at the upper end, and very few Winter Farms passed the 50,000 mark without hiving people off to create new communities elsewhere.

The governments of the nation-states were in a double bind. They knew the gruesome arithmetic of nuclear war and nuclear winter better than anyone, but they also saw the development of self-reliant Winter Farms as a challenge to their authority. This was especially the case in regions such as Europe, where the instruction to the urban populations in the event of nuclear war was often to stay put and die like brave citizens. More generally, if the national governments encouraged the development of self-reliant villages, they would be creating the infrastructure for their own demise. They would put themselves out of business, politically and fiscally. How would you tax voluntary labor, or collect revenue on a shirt made from local resources and given to the wearer without money changing hands? More fundamentally, how could you justify collecting taxes, when the nation-state had obviously failed in its primary responsibility of guaranteeing the defense of its citizens? But if the governments opposed the creation of the Winter Farms they would seem at best to be stifling enterprise and at worst to be wishing their people dead. A further complication was that military opponents suspected that winter farming on the other side was but a preparation for a nuclear attack.

The political and administrative apparatus of the nation-state was a finely tuned system for focusing praise and diffusing blame. What it found hard to deal with was indifference, when the public in ever growing numbers behaved as if the government and its defense programs had become, not hated, but irrelevant. In the outcome, some governments tried to take charge of the devolution by sponsoring it themselves, while others tolerated it, offering various degrees and kinds of help. Others again set up roadblocks around the cities and destroyed any rural Winter Farms they could find.

Farsighted villagers everywhere counted self-defense as part and parcel of survival. In the chaos following a nuclear war, improvident people from the cities and marauding soldiers would create a grave threat, and so might militarists in other Winter Farms. They also foresaw the day, even in peacetime, when desperate national governments would send tax collectors in battle tanks.

How the Winter Farms acquired their weapons determined the flavor of the revolution in the various countries. Where the purchase of machine guns and antitank missiles was unopposed or even aided by the authorities, the revolution tasted like an economic and social confection, with military trappings. At the other extreme, violent opposition from national governments politicized the revolution and turned it into a civil war. In these cases, the villagers followed the guerrilla principle of arming themselves with weapons captured from their attackers.

The intermediate situation was the trickiest, in countries where private arsenals were simply illegal and the villagers had no wish to provoke conflict. Here the military preparations were a clandestine affair of smuggled and homemade weapons and explosives. The explosives were especially important for creating instant antitank ditches and other physical barriers, should the need arise. The village militias conducted their drills and maneuvers with wooden weapons to fool the authorities, but everyone had to learn to shoot.

The news trickled back to the cities that the villagers were arming to defend their food supplies in the event of a nuclear winter. The remaining inhabitants of the cities then had the impression of a door closing on them. Either they must join the rush to the countryside or look to their own food supplies. By then the gruesome arithmetic was the subject of standard jokes, and whenever international relations took a turn for the better there was further amusement in city pubs about all the foolish folk who had left for no good reason. But in the end, nearly everyone with families decided to go, and the cities were as empty of children as if the Pied Piper had passed by.

Green Machines for Survival

During the darkest days of the nuclear winter in the Northern Hemisphere, living on Earth would be like occupying a gloomy and chilly planet far beyond the orbit of Mars. A reduction in the intensity of sunlight to 13 percent of its normal level would correspond with conditions in the asteroid belt. At 4 percent, you might as well be living on one of Jupiter's moons as far as solar energy was concerned. The sunlight would gradually return as the sky cleansed itself of soot, but to light up a ruined planet on which many plants, animals, and people would already be dead. The paralysis of transport and trade would reconfirm the sense of isolation, as if one's Winter Farm were a long rocket journey from Earth.

When it came to planning a green system to sustain life, during and after the nuclear winter, indigenous farmers knew better than anyone else the character of their land and its surroundings, and what plants and animals they supported. But nuclear winter was outside their experience and so were the problems of working within an armed camp surrounded by thousands of people, all of whom were keen to help. Too keen in some cases: anyone who had ever raised a rubber plant in his window thought he had arcane knowledge to contribute, and people predisposed to back-to-Nature, eco-agronomic theories of the good life were among the first to arrive at the sites of the Winter Farms, offering to defecate on the crops. Scientific guidance was badly needed.

The supreme virtue of biotechnology, as of life itself, lay in its capacity to create resources anywhere, out of sunlight, air, and water. That was why it had the leading scientific role in the revolution of the Winter Farms. As the emigration from the cities began, multidisciplinary groups of sympathetic experts sketched, computed, and in some cases tested by experiment the technical aids to survival. Except in the most complaisant nation-states and adaptive companies, the scientists worked unofficially and sometimes secretly. They circulated their suggestions by photocopies and word of mouth, and distributed their cultures of special-purpose bacteria in plastic bags.

Different scientific teams evolved their own packages of technology, and by the time the Winter Farms had adapted them to the local environments and their own ideas and prejudices, no two systems were alike. There were contrasts in style, too, with some communities concentrating austerely on worst-case policies for survival, and others aiming for the greatest prosperity and comfort in peacetime, in the belief that the healthier the system the more resilient it would be. But a number of features were tested by many of the Winter Farms, and widely adopted.

A switch of part of the available land to crops better able to withstand a chilling was the most direct action in response to the effects predicted for the nuclear winter. The cold, not the darkness, was the deadliest factor. Thus rice and maize gave way to wheat and barley wherever possible, and soya to peas. Another common adaptation to the expected cold was the construction of greenhouses for growing, not fancy salad crops, but staple foods. For many communities the most prized input from biotechnology was a microbial and chemical kit for turning plant wastes into tough transparent plastics for glazing the greenhouses. When that became available, the areas under "controlled-environment" agriculture grew as fast as human effort allowed. In targeted countries where blast and fire were a danger the Winter Farms kept large stockpiles of the sheeting in readiness for repairs. The most sophisticated greenhouses were used for cooling as well as warming, so that cold-resistant crops could grow better in hot climates.

The spread of greenhouses eased other expected problems of the nuclear winter. When the soot in the upper air suppressed the normal circulation of the atmosphere, it would trap poisonous fumes from the burning cities and factories close to ground level. In regions near to nuclear targets, radioactive fallout was a grave matter too. Even a thin membrane separating the crops and living quarters from these forms of air pollution could make the difference between life and death. In the best systems, air pumps powered by renewable fuels maintained an excess pressure of filtered air within the covered areas, so that any leaks were outward.

With control of the air went control of the water. The rains might fail in many places, so water conservation and recycling had a high priority. The nutrient-film technique for growing crops in gutters was sparing of water, and in greenhouses even the water transpired by the crops could be recaptured. Microbes and plants cleaned all waste water in purification systems and made it available for reuse, while emergency backup and fire-fighting tanks served for culturing algae and fish.

People lived underground in many of the Winter Farms. There were various reasons for doing so. In targeted countries the homes were blast-proof shelters, with air filters to exclude the fallout and the fumes, and these shelters naturally went below the surface. Elsewhere, going underground saved valuable land and heating energy, and also provided a ready-made defensive network of tunnels, in the Vietcong fashion. Communal buildings for daytime use stayed on the surface, but key workshops, biogas plants, and other microbial vats were usually underground, together with the gene banks in which the Winter Farms preserved many of the cultivated and natural plants of their regions.

Some crops grew underground. In the 1980s, Kenneth Edwards of Ariel Industries in England had reported high yields of tomatoes under low levels of light, using the second-generation nutrient-film technique in a project for growing plants indoors by artificial light. The light intensity was equivalent to only about 10 percent of normal daylight. The plants responded to rich nutrient solutions by doubling the amount of chlorophyll in their leaves, thus becoming more efficient collectors of the available light. Some of the Winter Farms adopted similar techniques to produce salad crops, and also medicinal plants selected from manuals of modernized herbal medicine, written for the winter farmers by helpful doctors and pharmacists. The dim cellars were also useful for preadapting seedlings to be grown on the surface at low light levels, during the dark phase of the nuclear winter.

Enterprising companies, and some of the Winter Farms themselves, mass-produced and marketed photovoltaic cells for generating electricity from daylight. The amorphous-silicon sheets helped to create large-scale emergency food-production systems using artificial light. These were located wholly underground, except for the solar-energy collectors spread out on the surface. Standby generators running on hydrogen or biofuels would keep the electric lights glowing when the sun went dark. Those who could afford these systems liked to claim that they had the ideal technical answer to nuclear winter, but for the human species as a whole it was microbiology that offered the key to safety.

"Make anything from anything," was the chief message from the biotechnologists to the winter farmers, as they preached the principle of interconvertability. All living and once-living matter was available for conversion into food, energy and organic materials, while any food, energy, and organic materials could support new growth of living things. It was technically absurd that anyone should die for want of calories as long as any log, waterweed, or cesspit remained within reach. An immature crop struck dead by the nuclear winter would remain as useful biomass.

The biotechnologists also cultured the necessary microorganisms and explained how to keep them going and avoid contamination. Yeasts for growing as food on many kinds of substances, methane-makers for the biogas tanks, nitrogen-fixers and pesticidal bacteria to replace the agrochemicals, single-cell algae for growing in water—these were basic items in every microbiological package. As the winter farmers grew more expert with their cultures and vats and immobilized cells they were clamoring for microbes and enzymes that opened the way to a do-it-yourself chemical industry based on lignocellulose, the stuff of wood and straw. Many microbiologists liked to end their homilies by saying: "If in doubt, make alcohol. It's a very efficient way of producing calories and if need be you can pass the nuclear winter in a drunken stupor."

Glorious Summer

The risk of a severe nuclear winter abated, though not because decaying nation-states gave up their nuclear weapons. Obsessively, like brain-damaged persons who had lost all rational control of their actions, they insisted on developing new weapons systems as the first use for the dwindling tax revenues. "Why are you running away?" one national leader asked. "Our new multi-beam Space Dreadnought will keep you safe forever."

The nuclear targeteers rewrote their lists to reduce the likely smoke pall. Oil refineries that had been priority targets since the 1940s were struck off, and the warhead yields assigned to city targets diminished. But the spy satellites revealed that both superpowers were installing missile silos inside oil refineries and cities in the hope of discouraging attacks upon them. So the target lists were soon restored, with the addition of some of the larger Winter Farms in the opponent's territory, on the grounds that they possessed well-armed militias.

The evacuation of the cities, and the rundown of stocks of paper, oil, and other flammable material concentrated in them, was the biggest factor in reducing the severity of any likely nuclear winter. Secret-service gossip told of the demented leader of an oil-rich state who was busy installing thermonuclear mines in his oil fields, in order to create a smoky Doomsday Machine. So the threat remained, as indeed it would for the remainder of the human species' tenure of the planet Earth. The feasibility of making nuclear weapons for setting the world on fire would never be forgotten.

Some people who had given up important jobs in the cities felt cheated when the years passed without the nuclear winter supervening. But they were a minority, and to many the new life seemed like an unending vacation, compared with their previous boring, specialized work and often lonely lives, whether in the cities or on the farms. Every little practical success was an occasion for celebration, and shared difficulties were not only easier to bear but more likely to be solved by someone's ingenuity.

Not since the world began had there been such an unleashing of latent talent and creativity as occurred during the establishment of the Winter Farms. Biotechnologists estimated that their subject advanced as much in two decades as it would have done in two centuries in ordinary circumstances. The winter farmers made good a huge backlog of botany and plant biochemistry. As they examined thousands of disregarded species in their local environments, they found many useful properties and products that the experts had overlooked. In helping to run the enzyme systems of the Winter Farms, everyone was a chemist of sorts. The gardeners became mechanics, and the mechanics, gardeners.

Creative high spirits found outlets in every direction, from tunnel paintings that rivaled Lascaux to genetic engineering of exquisite subtlety. The traditional dislike of technology imposed from outside gave way to an enthusiasm for homemade gadgets and systems. Computers were everywhere, and the countless millions of lines of new software sometimes contained gems that opened up new domains of practical application, fun and games, or philosophical enquiry. Every self-respecting Winter Farm had its video studio and exchanged its dramas and documentaries with other communities.

The greatest liberation came with the removal of the terrible burden of worldwide norms, which made anyone who had not won a Nobel prize, a Golden Disk, or an Olympic medal feel vaguely incompetent. A person who might trail far behind the field in the 100 meter sprint in the Olympics could still be the fastest athlete in his district and just the man to carry an antitank missile launcher. In the arts and sciences inhibitions fell away like scales from the eyes. Although a great deal of worthless material resulted, people enjoyed themselves and many a village Leonardo came to light.

The Misery Machines were largely brought under control. The Winter Farms, proof against fallout or man-made darkness, solved the riddle of the Doomsday Machine. Commandos in protective clothing attacked and destroyed a number of laboratories—one of them in a Winter Farm—that were suspected of making Doomsday Bugs. One nation-state succeeded in wiping out a million of its winter farmers with a chemical weapon, but it triggered a bloody revolution that ended in the deaths of the entire Establishment. As for the Big Brother Machine, tunneling gave protection from the eyes of the spy satellites, and the winter farmers had no reason to snoop on one another.

The bad habits that had led to the systematic misuse of science and technology virtually died with the nation-states, where decisions had been made by people hidden away in palaces and office blocks. The inhabitants of the Winter Farms could look a would-be perpetrator in the eye and say No. In exceptional cases where a Winter Farm achieved a consensus for creating potentially dangerous organisms, or attempting to apply genetic engineering to human beings, an alliance of neighboring communities would soon tell it to stop.

More positively, all of the cornucopias offered by modern science became directly useful to the dispersed communities. The robotics that pointed toward the Santa Claus Machine developed at the same accelerated pace as the Green Machines. People in coastal regions developed Ocean Cities, at first as mere piers extending from the shore, but later as free-floating green machines. When experienced groups hived off from the first generation of Winter Farms, they prided themselves on being able to live anywhere, and that was how the deep Sahara, the high Himalayas, and the continent of Antarctica came to be populated. The biggest bonus was coal, when people who had taken over disused mines as ready-made nuclear shelters perfected biotechnological systems that broke down the structure of the coal and turned it into the richest of all resources, after sunlight itself, for making food and materials.

In short, the burst of activity by people anxious to cope with the worst that the nuclear winter could do to them resulted in a glorious summer for the human species. Winter farmers in Third World countries suffered the most hardship during the great transition, for want of a few dollars to buy needed equipment, but biotechnology worked its miracles there, too, and the great gulf between the rich and poor nations was narrowed. Southern countries that took pride in escaping the panic found themselves stranded, technologically and socially, in the twentieth century. The governments of Argentina and Australia tried telling their people that it was their patriotic duty to decentralize, but anyone could see that was a contradiction in terms.

The greatest pride for the winter farmers was in their restoration of wildlife. The areas liberated by the implosion of cultivation into small, defendable places released large tracts of land for reforestation, and wherever possible the native trees were planted in mixed stands. The emergency committees earmarked them a potential source of biomass and also insisted on wide firebreaks.

That wonderful paradox, the man-made wilderness of the Evolution Machine, came into being as a huge laboratory-cum-playground. Ecological islands, planned introductions of exotic species, and occasional interventions by genetic engineers were all designed to maximize the diversity of species. There were always lively disputes about the reintroduction of the top predators, but those who said "Bring back the wolves!" (or the tigers or the leopards) usually won the argument.

The genetic engineers' finest hour came with the *Smilodon* experiment. Out of fossil material from the La Brea Tar Pits of California they reconstructed a living pride of large sabertooth cats and set them loose in the forests of North America. Being larger than lions, with canine teeth 20 centimeters long, they were judged the best deterrent to tax collectors ever invented.

Many a winter farmer liked to tell the children that everything they did was just a rehearsal for the day when the human species would go out to colonize Mars and the broad deserts of space. Certainly the Winter Farms were the ideal proving ground for the biotechnological and social systems that the space settlements would need, if they were to have any real chance of indefinite survival. By the time the Winter Farms had achieved a measure of secure affluence, space technology was a widespread hobby.

The most misleading statement ever made about the Swiss was that by Orson Welles, who said in a movie that all they ever invented was the cuckoo clock. In fact people from that land of villages won a string of Nobel prizes out of all proportion to the size of the population, most notably for chemistry and physiology. The industrial prowess of Switzerland was advertised as much by their exports of turbogenerators and fine chemicals as by their famous clocks and watches. The Swiss had little difficulty in getting their act together to tunnel through the Alps or create networks of railroads and highways. So it was with the world of Winter Farms: they were entirely capable of pooling resources to accomplish anything they liked.

There was therefore no reason for surprise when the first unofficial space launcher rose from the European heartland of winter farming. The craft was a curious hybrid of secondhand missile parts in a homemade airframe, and it nose-dived into the Baltic Sea. But the second one worked, and within a decade a spacecraft manned by winter farmers was threading its way through the grotesque space battle fleets of the erstwhile superpowers, like *Mayflower* through the navy of the Stuart kings.

Living in our global green machine on Mars, we still like to look back at the most beautiful planet of them all. Awareness of the dangerous history that brought us here leads us to cross our fingers before we switch on the orbital telescope, hoping that no sooty smudge will be disfiguring the Earth tonight. So far, so good. Some of the youngsters here are restless and talking of a journey to Barnard's Star, just as we used to chat about traveling to Mars.

The word from the asteroid belt is that dreadful experiments in human genetic engineering are in progress, aimed at making people who will be better adapted to life in zero gravity. We always feared that the human species would begin fragmenting in space, but even so it comes as a shock to hear of it happening. Those who opposed manipulations of life because they could be misapplied in *Homo sapiens* had a case. Other forebodings, about the use of engineered organisms in agriculture, were for the most part unwarranted, except in the matter of the recalcitrant mold invented to digest horny materials. Toenails and fingernails painted prophylactically in lurid colors are now our badge of freedom.

ADDITIONAL READING

This book draws on a wide variety of sources (interviews, meetings, books, journals, newspapers, and unpublished material), and a comprehensive bibliography would be cumbersome. The following listings give suggestions for further reading and also note the sources directly quoted in the text.

PARTS 1 AND 2: BEFORE THE REVOLUTION; POWERS OF LIGHT

On biotechnology in the 1980s:

FISHLOCK, D., and E. ANTÉBI. *Biotechnology: Strategies for Life.* Cambridge: MIT Press, 1986.

POSTGATE, J. *Microbes and Man.* Rev. ed. London and New York: Penguin, 1986.
ELKINGTON, J. *The Gene Factory.* London: Century, 1985.
YANCHINSKI, S. *Setting Genes to Work.* London: Viking, 1985.

More technical sources on biotechnology applied in agriculture:

SASSON, A. *Biotechnologies: Challenges and Promises.* Paris: UNESCO, 1984.
BLAXTER, K., and L. FOWDEN, eds. *Technology in the 1990s: Agriculture and Food.* London: Royal Society, 1985.
REXEN, F., and L. MUNCK. *Cereal Crops for Industrial Use in Europe.* Brussels: Commission of the European Communities, 1984.
TODD, N. J., and J. TODD. *Bioshelters, Ocean Arks, City Farming.* San Francisco: Sierra Club, 1984.

Appraisals by the Office of Technology Assessment of the U.S. Congress, Washington D.C., various titles, and by the Food and Agriculture Organization of the UN, Rome, various titles, are very useful; so are global overviews from the Worldwatch Institute, Washington D.C., for example in L. R. Brown and others, *State of the World,* New York and London: Norton 1984, 1985, and 1986.

Directly quoted sources in alphabetical order are:

Commission of the European Communities (definition of biotechnology) "Biotechnology in the Community" document COM(83) 672 final/2—Annex, Oct. 3, 1983; Freeman J. Dyson, *Disturbing the Universe,* New York: Harper and Row, 1979; European Council of Chemical Manufacturers' Federations, "Bioethanol—A Viable Use of Renewable Resources?" CEFIC position paper, Oct. 1985; L. Garrett, article reprinted in University of Georgia publication, 1985; Bob Geldof, press and TV reports of his visit to European Parliament, 1985; J. B. S. Haldane, *Daedalus,* London: Kegan Paul, 1925; G. Junne, seminar paper, Mexico, Nov. 30, 1984; C. W. Lewis, *The Use of Dynamic Systems Analysis to Assess the Potential for Enhanced Output in the Rural Communities of Developing Countries,* Tokyo and Paris: United Nations University, 1985; A. L. Morton, *The*

English Utopia, London: Lawrence and Wishart, 1978; K.-H. Narjes, speech to Centre for European Studies, Nov. 7, 1985; K. Sargeant, lecture, Cambridge, Sep. 3, 1985; J. Swift, *Gulliver's Travels,* original 1726, reprinted London and New York: Penguin, 1967.

PART 3 AND POSTSCRIPT: POWERS OF DARKNESS; THE WINTER FARMS

On nuclear winter:

PETERSON, J., and D. HINRICHSEN, eds. *The Aftermath.* Oxford: Pergamon, 1982.

PITTOCK, A. B., and others, eds. *Environmental Consequences of Nuclear War,* Vol. 1 (Physical & Atmospheric Effects). Chichester, New York, etc.: Wiley, 1986.

HARWELL, M. A., and T. C. HUTCHINSON. *Environmental Consequences of Nuclear War,* Vol. 2 (Ecological and Agricultural Effects). Chichester, New York, etc.: Wiley 1985.

On the history of states:

MCNEILL, W. H., *A World History.* Oxford, New York, etc.: Oxford University Press, 1979.

CALDER, N., *Timescale.* New York: Viking, 1983.

On the legitimacy of science:

MAXWELL, N., *From Knowledge to Wisdom.* Oxford: Blackwell, 1984.

RYLE, M., letter to C. Chagas dated Feb. 24, 1983, published by A. Rudolf and M. Rowan Robinson in *New Scientist,* Vol. 105, Feb. 14 1985, p. 36.

On social transformations:

MANUEL, F. E., and F. P. MANUEL. *Utopian Thought in the Western World.* Oxford: Blackwell, 1979.

SCHUMACHER, E. F., *Small Is Beautiful.* New York: Harper Torchbooks, 1973.

SALE, K. *Dwellers in the Land.* San Francisco: Sierra Club, 1985.

204 THE GREEN MACHINES

On Kropotkin:

KROPOTKIN, P. *Fields, Factories and Workshops Tomorrow.* Original 1892; reprinted London: Allen and Unwin, 1974.
KROPOTKIN, P. *Mutual Aid.* original 1902; reprinted London: Allan Lane, 1972.
WOODCOCK, G. *Anarchism.* Original 1962; reprinted with postscript London and New York: Penguin, 1975.

On evolution and behavior:

SMITH, J. MAYNARD, ed. *Evolution Now.* London: Nature/Macmillan, 1982.
WILSON, E. O. *On Human Nature.* Cambridge: Harvard University Press, 1978.

On Switzerland:

McPHEE, J. *La Place de la Concorde Suisse.* New York: Farrar, Straus and Giroux, 1984.
LUCK, J. M., and others, eds. *Modern Switzerland.* Palo Alto: SPOSS, 1978.

Directly quoted sources in alphabetical order are:

M. Bookchin in R. Merrill (ed.), *Radical Agriculture,* New York: New York University Press, 1976; G. K. Chesterton, *The Napoleon of Notting Hill,* original 1904, reprinted London, New York: Penguin, 1946; W. S. Churchill, quoted by Donald Kerr; Y. Dror, *Crazy States,* Millwood, NY: Krauss Reprints, 1970; J. Elkington, *The Gene Factory,* as above; S. Hoggart, *The Observer* (London) Sep. 22, 1985; S. Johnson, *Oxford Dictionary of Quotations,* London, New York, etc.: Oxford University Press, 1953; P. Kropotkin (on crabs and on conscience) *Mutual Aid,* as above; _____(on invention) *Fields, Factories and Workshops Tomorrow,* as above; _____(on dictators) quoted in Woodcock, *Anarchism,* as above; F. E. Manuel and F. P. Manuel, *Utopian Thought in the Western World,* as above; N. Maxwell, *From Knowledge to Wisdom,* as above; J. Naisbitt, *Megatrends,* New York: Warner, 1982; *New York Times* editorial, Sept. 29 1985; Pharmacia advertisement published (e.g.) in *Nature,* 1985; K. Sale, *Human Scale,* New York: Coward-McCann, 1980;

G. B. Shaw, quoted in Woodcock, *Anarchism,* as above; A. Toffler, *The Third Wave,* New York: William Morrow and Company, Inc., 1976; A. J. Toynbee, "The Reluctant Death of Sovereignty" in *The Center Magazine,* Center for the study of Democratic Institutions, Santa Barbara, undated reprint; H. G. Wells, "The Man of the Year Million"; reprinted in W. W. Wagar, ed. *H. G. Wells: Journalism and Prophecy,* Boston: Houghton Mifflin, Inc. 1964.